SOUL
SEARCHERS

"The First Mission"

DAVEY G. ROBERSON

DiAnn,

May you always be
surrounded by love!

Davey

Destiny Publishing

North Little Rock, Arkansas

Destiny Publishing, P.O. Box 94436

North Little Rock, AR 72190

Printed in the United States of America

First Printing

ISBN 0-9656344-0-X

Illustrations by Bill Reames

**Dedicated to the loving memory of my mother,
"Jean"**

When God Calls

Father

A sadness creeps into my heart
because I thought we'd never part.
The nights pass slowly for me, dear,
because you are no longer near.

I lie awake and wonder how
this could happen to me right now.
Life was good and I was content
in thinking you were heaven sent.

There was no way for me to know
just when it was your time to go.
We couldn't know when it would end
so we have nothing to defend.

The world continues to revolve
but my loss is hard to resolve.
Life continues without you, love,
because I know you are above.

I must wait till my time is done
before we are again as one.
You are gone but your love is here
inside me and in every tear.

I miss you dearly but I know
I will be with you when I go.
Sleep peacefully and wait to see
me join you when God comes for me.

Mother

A sadness creeps into your heart
because you thought we'd never part.
The nights pass slowly for you, dear,
because I am no longer near.

You lie awake and wonder how
this could happen to you right now.
Life was good and you were content
in thinking I was heaven sent.

There was no way for you to know
just when it was my time to go.
We couldn't know when it would end
so we have nothing to defend.

The world continues to revolve
but your loss is hard to resolve.
Life continues without me, love,
because you know I am above.

You must wait till your time is done
before we are again as one.
I am gone but my love is there
inside you and in every tear.

You miss me dearly but you know
you will be with me when you go.
I sleep in peace and wait for you
to join me when God asks you to.

To Mom and Dad with all my love.

your son,
Davey

CONTENTS

CONTENTS

PROLOGUE

My name is Daniel. I lived many, many years ago. I lived my life much as any other person. I was born into the world, lived life, and finally died. What I didn't know all during my life was what would come next.

I died on September 12, 2020. I awoke again in the year 3473. I was guided in the ways of the New World by my Guide, Robert. Robert was born to the New World in 2216, some thousand plus years after the end of the Old World. He became a Saver and accomplished many Soul Saver missions during those 1,200 years. I was only one of many he saved.

Robert guided me in the ways of the New World. I toured everything, was shown everything, and learned about everything imaginable. I spent 20 years with Robert before I completely understood the New World. Time has very little meaning in the New World. Only the past, specifically the Old World past, is strictly kept track of in terms of years.

In general terms the New World is Heaven. I learned that the Old World passed away in the year 2187. Man, on Earth, had driven himself to near self destruction. Mankind was nearly on the edge of creating the perfect world. Most known diseases had been conquered and life spans were greatly lengthened. Then, man discovered and developed the means to replicate himself in laboratories. Many experiments were carried out in order to discover a means to transplant a person's essence into the new bodies. The scramble to live forever began and created a madness in the world.

Self concern and lack of compassion for others grew until chaos ruled the world. Fighting erupted between those to be transplanted and the ones who were passed over. Pursuit of lasting life became an overpowering desire allowing greed and jealousy to engulf mankind. The fighting turned into global warfare and man destroyed the civilization it took over two thousand years to build. The Earth was in ruin. The time of the Apocalypse came.

The world was rebuilt with Divine Intervention creating a New World from the ashes of the Old World. Counsels were appointed by The Fathers to rule over the New World. They appointed members of the Counsels from those who kept themselves from falling into the madness man had created. Through the wise guidance of the Counsels and The Fathers, mankind was taught to live in harmony with one another and keep the New World at peace.

There are many things about the New World that Pre-Life souls do not know or understand. I have placed the following thoughts and events on paper in hope of relieving fears, causing a greater understanding, providing comfort, and most importantly, create hope for those that are in need.

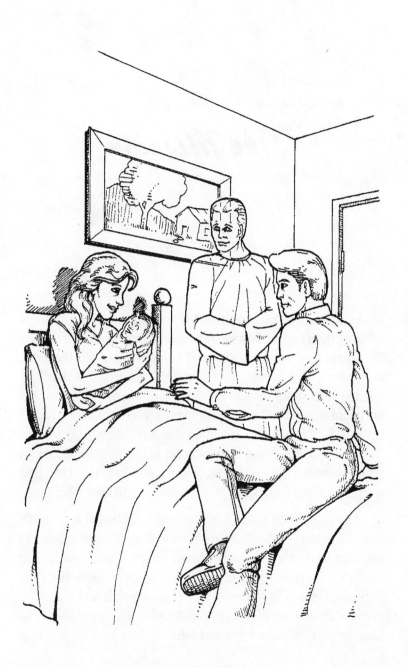

The Mission

I studied the Travel-Pod as I slowly approached, my steps echoing in my ears. My heart began pounding steadily faster the nearer I came. I wondered if my Saver had felt the same excitement that I was now feeling. Since my ReBirth, I learned everything about the Soul Searchers. The process intrigued me from the very moment I was told about how I came to be Reborn. It isn't often that a New Born becomes a Saver. I had the choice of any career in the New World, but a Saver is what I wanted to be. Now I was beginning my first assignment and feelings of wonder and excitement filled me.

The process of placing a Saver with a Chosen is a totally random process. Each Saver's record is selected randomly and matched to a Chosen's record which is also selected at random. A random selection process determines the time period a Chosen is returned to. The selection and matching process for my mission was completed in a nanosecond. The lengthy part came as I studied what history I could find that applied to my Chosen. I greedily poured over every bit of information, trying to memorize everything I found. It didn't take long to learn all I needed to know because my Chosen had a very short history. Within a week, the Departure time was set and I was ready to begin my first mission.

Nearing the Travel-Pod, I noticed how the cleanliness of the New World still impressed me. Everything sparkled like clear fresh water, looking ice cold but emitting warmth. As I stepped into the transportation chamber and heard the hissing of the door sliding closed, my mind turned to my Chosen. Critical facts rapidly flashed through my mind. Name: Sarah Jean Robinson. Date, time and location of birth: April 17, 1955, 06:30, small farm, near Rantoul, Illinois. Date, time, and location of death: June 22, 1980, 08:47, Chicago, Illinois. The times of birth and death were taken from historical records and I hoped they were accurate. I would now study her brief life in great detail, recording and transmitting every second of her life for the time of her ReBirth in the New World.

The time period and location of Sarah closely matched that of my own Pre-Life. I was nearly 2 years old at the time of her birth and existed within 100 miles of her nearly all of my Pre-Life. However, my Pre-Life continued for 40 years after her death. It was a strange coincidence, one that had never occurred in the history of the Soul Searchers. This was of great concern to the Soul Searcher Counsel and they were very upset that I would be performing the mission so near to myself and people I knew. However, they did not have the power to cancel the mission. Only The Fathers could cancel a Saver mission.

The Fathers watch over and care for the New World.

Without their wisdom and guidance, mankind would slip back into old ways. They are always just and fair in any matter that comes before them. My mission was referred to them. They studied my history as well as the information that was available on Sarah. After days of contemplation and study, The Fathers decided to allow the mission to continue as scheduled. My Chosen is Sarah and I am her Saver.

As the countdown to Soul Watch began, I was extremely anxious. I would now spend the next 25 odd years in close proximity to my Chosen, Sarah. I felt a surge of pride and confidence. I knew my mission would be successful. I knew I could capture and save Sarah. The course was set. The Soul Watch was placed into action as the counter reached zero. My mind was racing, my heart was pounding, my very soul was on fire.

A numbness that had been previously described overcame me. I felt as if I were being rapidly lifted upward toward the sky and I felt my own weight bearing down on me. Then, just as suddenly as it began, the lifting ceased. The numbness vanished and the weight I felt was lifted. I could see the dark sky filled with stars shining above me. The area in which I found myself was an empty field, somewhat barren. The landscape surrounding me was filled with shadows. I could taste and smell the cool Spring morning approaching.

Remote locations were always selected as appearance sights. This was done in order to ensure Pre-Life souls didn't accidentally discover a Traveler. I had been told of incidents where Travelers had been seen appearing. Often times, these appearances were mistaken as the arrival of divinity. There were many sites around the world where a Traveler appeared and were mistakenly preserved as holy places. I took note of the fact that there was no one anywhere near me as I looked around to establish my bearings.

A worn country road was nearby and I crossed the field to follow the road into the small town. I knew this place, not in this time, but as it would be nearly twenty years from now. Memories of my Pre-Life filled me, warming me. Familiar buildings and surroundings made me feel at home. I glanced at my chronometer and realized that it was time to perform necessary tasks.

April 17, 1955, 05:00 softly glowed in a light green color. This was the present time. Then I checked the programmed departure time. June 22, 1980, 08:52 glowed in a soft amber. The calculated departure time was 5 minutes past Sarah's known time of death. If I could not capture her by that time, Sarah's soul could be lost for a very long time. My failure would place her in the hands of the Lost Soul Searchers and it could take eons before they could capture and save her. I must not fail Sarah!

I verified Invisibility by standing in front of a small cafe. No reflection of my existence was visible in the window. Next, I tested Fluidity by passing through the cafe door. I was completely fluid and passed through the door with ease. It felt strange to walk through such objects even though I understood the phenomena. I also knew the importance of remaining in this state. Invisibility and Fluidity allowed a Saver to remain in close proximity of a Chosen and gather every detail of their Pre-Life. So far, no Saver was ever detected by a Chosen while on a mission.

I noticed a light near the rear of the cafe and heard the clattering of dishes. Standing there, putting dishes away was a middle aged woman wearing a long, clean, white apron. She appeared happy in her task, singing softly as she worked. This was the perfect opportunity to check Sound Absorption. I called out to her, "Hello, can you hear me?" There was no response as she continued working and singing. I clapped my hands together and again, she continued about her work. Sound Absorption was working.

I moved out to the street and began programming the chronometer to indicate that Invisibility, Fluidity, and Sound Absorption were functioning. This action set an auto-alarm that would instantly transport me back to the Starting Point should any or all of the functions fail. If, for some reason, the alarm had not been set within the first two hours of the mission, the return command would have automatically transported me back. Any failure in the 3 functions would end the mission and Sarah would be returned to the Chosen waiting list, or worse, be lost. I must not fail for Sarah's sake. Her loss would be unbearable to me. I must complete the observation, transfer all data, and successfully capture Sarah. Nothing short of complete success would suffice.

After verifications were completed and the auto-alarm set, it was time to locate Sarah. The chronometer indicated one hour until her birth. Even though her time of birth was accurately determined from Seeker records, I felt an urgency to get to her birth place. I knew the general area and felt I must hurry to get there. I knew that following the railroad tracks would be the fastest course as I hurried down the street to the railway. The route to Sarah flashed in my mind.

A sense of urgency tugged at me as I walked along the quiet tracks. The crossroad I needed came into view after about 40 minutes. Only 20 minutes to reach Sarah! I scolded myself for taking too much time in town. I cut across an open field to intersect the gravel road which lead to Sarah and quickened my pace to jump over the small ditch. Only 15 minutes to reach Sarah! The lane leading to her birthplace was soon upon me and I rushed along it toward the small farmhouse. I quickly took note to ensure I was at the proper place. I slowed a bit as I saw a dark car parked in front of the house. I noticed an MD card on the dashboard and knew the doctor had already arrived. I stopped briefly to glance at my chronometer. One minute left! Sarah's birth was imminent.

I hastened my approach and heard a man saying, "Hurry, the baby is coming, bring me a sheet." At that, I rushed into the house and attempted to locate Sarah's mother. I heard moaning from the second floor and raced up the stairs. Quickly, I checked each room until I found her.

The bedroom was full of activity. The doctor was sitting on the bed in front of Sarah's mother. Sarah's father was standing to the side, gently squeezing her hand. The nurse was making preparations to clean and clothe Sarah. The doctor quietly said, "Push, Marge." "Push hard." "The baby is coming, I can see the head." "Marge, push now!"

I reached for my chronometer and activated the record command. Sarah's life was beginning! Every second of her life is precious and must be recorded to ensure a complete Re-Birth Process. My work for the next 25 odd years had begun. I would be with Sarah every second until her Pre-Life ended. I would then capture and transport her back with me to begin the New Life Process.

Sarah entered the world and the doctor said, "Marge, you have a beautiful baby girl." Marge began to cry and held the baby close as the doctor cut the umbilical cord. Marge looked at her female child and silently named her. She then gazed at her husband and asked, "Bill, isn't Sarah beautiful?"

I moved in close to where I could reach Sarah and extract a tiny amount of her blood, skin, and hair. I placed my arm across her tiny body and touched the genome receptacle on my chronometer to her thigh. I was startled for a second when I touched her because Sarah felt the extraction. She winced slightly and kicked out at the intrusion.

The receptacle indicator glowed green, indicating that enough material had been extracted. The next step was to transmit the material to the Growth Division. The laboratory location and time were preset within the receptacle. I verified the coordinates and activated the send command. Sarah's DNA would be extracted from the transported material and work on her New Life body would begin. Her New Life body would grow to the Perfection Point and remain isolated and prepared for the day I would return, carrying Sarah to her New Life.

Sensing Discovery

Time is a strange and wonderful thing. Sometimes it seems to pass so slowly, taking what seems eons for a second to pass. At other times, a whole year appears to pass in a nanosecond. Our perception of time moving is dependent on many circumstances, such as how we feel, what we are doing, and who we are with. Everyone experiences these passages of time throughout their life.

Being a Saver, especially one on a mission, brings on an added dimension. A Saver is completely alone and can only witness others. There is sight and sound, but no touch, no feeling other than our own. "It takes a special person to be a Saver." my Guide told me. Being alone with oneself would be lonely except for the caring of others and the knowledge that others are near.

I knew, before becoming a Saver, that I could be alone in myself. I had been that way during so much of my Pre-Life. That is why I, a New Born, was allowed to become a Saver. I also knew I could be alone and carry out the task of recording a Chosen. Besides, loneliness did not exist with Sarah. Being near her, watching her grow and learn, and sharing in her experiences made me very happy. Sharing with a Chosen is necessary in order to guide them in the New World. Being a Soul Searcher is a great joy.

In looking back, the past 5 years have passed quickly. I have been sending Sarah's history to the Historians regularly, allowing them to place her feelings and experiences into her growing body. I can picture her there as well as I can see her here. Both bodies growing, learning, and experiencing life. One so full of life and the other, empty and sheltered in the Birth Place, awaiting a New Life. Each separate, yet both the same.

The Birth Place is really a growing room. Each Chosen's New Life body grows and matures there waiting for the Pre-Life to end and the New Life to begin. They are exposed to the exact surroundings and feelings in that room as they were in their Pre-Life. It was explained to me that it must be as exact as possible in order for the New Life to begin where the Pre-Life ended. This way the Chosen would feel no loss when they were Reborn into the New World. They awake to familiar faces and in the presence of their Saver. Loved ones from their Pre-Life are usually there to welcome them and to provide comfort. The Saver then acts as a Guide, teaching them about the New World.

Much of Sarah's history I reviewed in the New World came from her great-grandmother. Sarah called her Nanna. I looked at Sarah as Nanna entered the room. "Nanna!", she cried, as she ran toward Nanna with her arms outstretched. Nanna gathered Sarah in her arms and hugged her dearly.

I knew Nanna would be leaving Sarah soon. Only another week and Nanna would die. I also knew another Saver was with Nanna and would guide her to her New Life. Every person I could see also had a Saver, each from a different time and place. We could not see, hear, or touch each other but we knew each other were there. It warmed my heart to know Nanna was being taken care of and would be saved. I also knew that Nanna would be in the Birth Place when Sarah awoke to her New Life. The task of Nanna's Saver was nearly at an end. Her Observation would now lead to her ReBirth. It was a comfort to know the commitment that particular Saver made to Nanna.

Sarah's life up till her fifth birthday was not very eventful. She grew and learned just as any other child. Her mannerisms were the same as any normal five year old. However, there seemed to be a uniqueness about her. I just couldn't pinpoint what it was. I felt the uniqueness in her history and didn't really understand it until the day of her fifth birthday.

Things were normal as Nanna entered the room that day and Sarah rushed to greet her. But, Sarah began to cry as Nanna hugged her. "What's wrong, Sarah?" asked Nanna. Sarah sobbed, "Oh, Nanna." "Why must you leave?" Nanna comforted Sarah, saying "Why Sarah, I've just arrived." "I'm not leaving." Sarah told her "But, Nanna." "You will be leaving soon and I won't see you again for a very long time." Nanna tried to console Sarah as she smoothed back the lengthy blonde hair from her face. "Sarah," she said, "Even if I leave you, I will still always be with you." She placed her finger to Sarah's chest and said, "I will always be here, in your heart." Nanna then gave Sarah a hug and led her to where the birthday cake and presents were waiting.

As I watched the proceedings, I dwelt on the uniqueness I felt in Sarah's history and what had just transpired. The thought suddenly dawned on me, "She knows!" "Sarah knows Nanna will be dying shortly." Her uniqueness was now revealed to me. Somehow Sarah sensed the departure of her Nanna. As I reflected back on the past five years, I remembered another event that Sarah sensed.

When Sarah was just past three years old she stared in my direction for what seemed the longest time. At first I thought she was noticing something behind me. Her face looked inquisitive and I turned to look behind me. Nothing was there except an open window with the curtains fluttering from the breeze. When I looked back, she was playing normally. At the time I thought she must have been daydreaming. It now came to me, "She sensed my presence somehow."

My immediate reaction was to recheck my Invisibility, Fluidity, and Sound Absorption. Relief washed through me as I determined that all 3 functions were working properly. I mentally noted the events and kept watch for any further indications that Sarah sensed me.

The following week passed as any other, but ended in sorrow for Sarah and her family. Nanna's time had come. I felt a sadness at her passing from this world and also felt jubilance, knowing her ReBirth was at hand. I knew another successful Saver mission had been completed. Another soul had been saved!

At Nanna's funeral, my attention turned to little Sarah. She was wearing a plain dark brown dress her mother had made. I watched as she approached the coffin where Nanna lay. There were no tears in her eyes, only a longing look. She stood on her tiptoes, peering over the coffin edge at Nanna.

Then she reached as best she could and touched Nanna's hand. "I will see you again soon, Nanna." she whispered. It appeared that somehow, Sarah sensed that Nanna was safe and they would see one another again. I made note of this event and filed it away in my mind with her other special sensing events.

Sarah's Tragedy

Time once again passed quietly and uneventfully. Sarah's seventh birthday came and went and the calm Spring turned into a sweltering Summer. This was the summer of another tragedy for Sarah.

July 16, 1962 dawned bright and sunny. It seemed just like any other July morning. However, this morning would be very different and forever change the life of the little girl Sarah. She wasn't aware of the events that would take place. No one knew, not even me. There was nothing in Sarah's history about this horrible day.

I began the day the same as every day I spent with Sarah. On this day, I watched as she slept and began to think of my own Pre-Life. Today was my ninth birthday in my Pre-Life. I thought back on how much fun I had on this day, playing and having my party. At that time in my existence I had no concept of the events that would unfold in Sarah's life on this day. I knew I shouldn't dwell on this as my Pre-Life was taking place elsewhere at this very moment. I now knew why the Soul Searcher Counsel had been concerned. I had a great yearning to leave Sarah and see myself and my family as we were on this day. I shook these feelings off and once again concentrated on Sarah.

My attention turned back to Sarah as she stirred from her sleep. She gently rubbed the sleep from her blue eyes with the back of her hand and sat up in bed. She stretched out her arms as if to hug the whole world and yawned a final yawn. Then she slowly climbed out of her bed and walked to the doorway of her bedroom. She paused briefly, straightening her long blonde hair and her long yellow nightgown. The hem of her nightgown was dragging on the floor, so she pulled it up slightly and held it up with one hand. She entered the hallway and I thought she was going to the bathroom as she normally did. Instead, she turned toward the stairway and took one step down.

Marge must have heard her rustlings and said, "Sarah, don't forget to brush your teeth before coming down for breakfast." A look of realization came over Sarah's face and she turned to return up the step she had taken. As she turned, she let go of her long nightgown to hold the banister. When she raised her foot to step up to the hallway floor, her big toe caught in the hem of her nightgown. Instinctively, she let go of the banister and reached down to free her toe from the nightgown.

As Sarah started reaching down to her foot, she lost her balance. She tried to recover her balance by reaching for the banister. Her hand reached out, but she was twisted slightly and only her fingertips brushed the banister. Sarah screamed as she began falling, tumbling down the flight of stairs. My heart jumped into my throat and I ran down the stairs to where Sarah was lying. As I looked at her tiny twisted body, Marge came running from the kitchen. She had heard the scream and the tumbling of Sarah's body down the stairs.

I could only stand and watch in horror, unable to do anything. Marge looked at her daughter and began sobbing, "Oh no, NO!" Tears were running down her cheeks as she knelt down to check Sarah. She shouted "Bill, come here." "Hurry!"

Bill had been in the barn, repairing the tractor. He was approaching the house when he heard Marge calling to him to hurry. Her voice concerned him and he immediately rushed into the house where he saw Marge kneeling at the foot of the stairway and heard her sobbing. As he came closer, he saw his daughter lying twisted on the floor.

Bill looked at Sarah lying at the foot of the stairs with her right arm lying beneath her limp body. Blood was slowly oozing from her nose and left ear, creating a dark pool on the floor. Her eyes were closed. He bent over Sarah, listened intently and stared at her chest. He could hear her shallow breathing and see her chest rise and fall. "Thank God, she's alive." he whispered to himself.

I watched all of this somberly. It saddened me to see Sarah lying there and I felt Bill and Marge's concern and worry. Even though I knew Sarah would survive this fall, I had no idea how it would affect her life. All I could do for Sarah was to stand silently by her and record the event for her New Life.

Bill carefully gathered his daughter into his arms and stood up. He started for the front door and motioned to

Marge to open the front screen door. Bill carried Sarah outside and around the pickup truck. "Open the door and get in, Marge." he said. Marge opened the door of the light blue truck and climbed into the seat, tears streaming down her face. Bill cautiously placed Sarah into his wife's arms, closed the door, and rounded the front of the pickup. He opened his door and climbed into his seat.

The engine came to life as he turned the ignition key. He placed the truck into motion and drove down the lane to the gravel road in front of the farmhouse. Bill drove hurriedly, but cautiously to the hospital. Time seemed to stand still as they traveled along the highway, but they finally arrived at the emergency room entrance of the hospital.

Bill stopped the truck, quickly got out, and was opening Marge's door in a matter of seconds. He took Sarah from her mother's arms and rushed into the hospital. "Help, I need help!" "My daughter needs help!" he shouted anxiously as he approached the desk.

The nurse saw Bill quickly approaching, holding his limp daughter, and immediately lead him to a vacant cubicle. The nurse told Bill to lay Sarah on the bed. She performed a quick examination of Sarah and then summoned the on duty doctor.

The doctor pushed aside the curtain, entered the cubicle and asked "What happened here?" Bill related to the doctor how he found Sarah at the foot of the stairway. Bill said, "She must have fallen and tumbled down the stairs." He sadly watched the doctor probe and examine his darling little girl. Bill kept whispering to himself, over and over, "Please be all right, Sarah." "Don't leave us Sarah." "Don't leave us."

As the doctor finished examining Sarah, Bill asked, "Is she going to be all right, doctor?" The doctor looked at Bill somberly and said "I don't know, I just don't know yet." The doctor continued looking at both Bill and Marge as he spoke, "It appears she has a skull fracture and her right arm is broken." "We will need to take x-rays to determine the extent of her head injuries." "Then we can better determine her condition." The doctor tried as best he could to comfort Bill and Marge before he left instructions with the nurse and went on to his next patient. As he left, he told them, "We will do everything we can for your little girl." "When we get her x-rays, we will know more."

Bill and Marge sat, stunned, in the waiting area. They both displayed how helpless they were in this situation. Both had an expression on their face that I read to mean "How could something like this happen?" The only thing they were able to do was stare into nothingness, hold each other, and cry with one another.

I followed Sarah everywhere they took her. The nurses handled Sarah with delicacy and great care, like a fragile flower. They cleaned the blood from her face, exposing bruises on her cheeks and forehead. Her blood stained gown was removed and she was draped in a fresh hospital garment. Then Sarah was wheeled from the emergency room cubicle to the x-ray department. Sarah appeared so tiny on the large gurney. Sweet Sarah!

Sarah was unaware of the nurses and the cold x-ray table. They placed her there like a little rag doll, arranging her head and body to begin the series of x-rays. Since the doctor wanted to check Sarah's skull fracture immediately, they positioned the machine over her head first. When the film was exposed, it was rushed for processing and sent to the doctor. Other x-rays located the break in her right arm. The break was set and her arm placed in a cast.

I stood, silent and invisible, recording everything. I knew Sarah would live and that provided some comfort to me as I watched, totally helpless. I wanted to tell everyone that she would be all right, to comfort Bill and Marge.

The loneliness and helplessness was part of being a Saver. These feelings are why many don't choose to become a Saver. I knew I could handle these, as did the Searcher Counsel. Otherwise, I would not be here now. I had been tested in this area many times and knew how difficult it would be. A Saver knows these feelings and overcomes them by knowing everything will be so much better when the mission is successfully completed. The anticipated feelings of elation at the conclusion of the Observation and ReBirth of the Chosen far outweigh feelings of loneliness or helplessness.

Sarah was placed in a normal hospital room, awaiting the doctors evaluation of her x-rays. She slept silently, all vital signs being regularly monitored by the on duty nurse. Bill and Marge sat solemn and quiet, staring at their little girl. Their attention was drawn from Sarah when Doctor Adams entered the room.

Doctor Adams entered the darkened room and quickly checked Sarah before turning to Bill and Marge. He saw the anticipation in their eyes and expressions. He appeared to hesitate a moment to collect his thoughts.

When Doctor Adams spoke, it was in a low, determined voice. "Bill." "Marge." he began, "I've studied Sarah's skull x-rays and it isn't good." Upon hearing this, Marge began sobbing. Bill hugged her close to him and said, "Go on Jim." "Tell us all you know."

Jim Adams had been a friend of Bill Robinson most of his life. He continued, wringing his hands, "Besides her broken arm and minor bruising, Sarah has a serious head injury." Tears came to Bill Robinson's eyes as Marge cupped her hands to her face and gasped. "She appears to have suffered extreme bleeding in the area controlling optic functions." "If Sarah pulls through..." He hesitated as a lump came to his throat, "If she survives the injury, I fear she will be blind." Jim Adams then knelt down before Bill and Marge Robinson, his friends, and shared their grief. He hugged them both tightly as all three of them cried together.

I stood in shock. Did that mean Sarah would not be blind, or was blindness just not in the available records? My mind analyzed all the possibilities, but I was unable to determine what would happen as far as Sarah's vision was concerned. I could only wait, as Bill and Marge waited, to learn what the outcome would be.

Survival

More than two weeks had gone by since Sarah's accident. Time seemed to move slowly, taking what appeared to be forever for each day to pass. Bill worked the farm during the day and would come to the hospital in the evening to stay with Sarah. Marge watched over her daughter from early morning until Bill arrived in the evening. They would spend about an hour with each other in the morning and again in the evening. They would discuss the days activities as they stood side by side at the foot of Sarah's bed, watching her. Then they would hug each other tightly for a few minutes and kiss one another good-bye.

Sarah finally awoke during the early morning of August third. I was startled a bit, not expecting to hear anything, when I heard a faint, "Who are you?" "Where am I?" The voice was unmistakably Sarah's. I looked at her and then quickly glanced at Bill. He had nodded off and hadn't heard Sarah. It was difficult to see in the subdued light and I moved closer to Sarah. Again she asked, "Who are you?" and turned her head in my direction. I was surprised when I realized she was talking to me! She repeated her question in a louder and frightened voice, "Who are you?" This time, Sarah's voice stirred Bill from his sleep.

Bill roused from his sleep and said, "Sarah, its daddy." "I'm here." He moved to the side of the bed opposite me. Sarah turned her head as she heard her father's voice and asked, "Daddy?" "Where are you, daddy?" Bill pressed the button for the nurse and said, "I'm here, baby." "Daddy's right here." He took her hand in his and switched on the bedside lamp.

The nurse heard the buzz of the signal and peered down the hallway. The light above room 104 was on. She knew Sarah Robinson was there and started walking down the hall to her room.

I watched as Bill reached out and took Sarah's tiny hand in his. "Sarah." "Oh my Sarah." he whispered. I was a bit dumbfounded by Sarah's reaction when she awoke. Was she merely confused or had she sensed my presence? As soon as the question passed through my mind it was answered. Sarah asked, "Daddy, who's that man?"

Bill answered, "What man, Sarah?" "I'm the only one here." Bill looked up as the door opened. "What is it, Mr. Robinson?" asked the nurse. "She's awake." he replied. The nurse passed through me to get to Sarah, something I still hadn't gotten completely used to. I immediately moved around to the foot of the bed to get a better view, watching the nurse check Sarah's pulse and peer into her eyes. Bill was also watching the nurse when she asked, "Sarah, how do you feel, honey?"

Sarah turned her head toward the nurse and said, "I feel okay." "Who are you?" "I'm Sally, Sarah." came the reply. "But, why can't I see you?" asked Sarah. The nurse looked up at Bill and shook her head sideways, indicating to him that Sarah's eyes were unseeing. Bill silently answered the nurse that he understood by slowly nodding his head up and down, his face showing a saddened look, tears welling up in his eyes.

During the next week, many tests and head x-rays were taken on Sarah. Doctor Adams consulted with the most knowledgeable brain specialists he could find. Each, in turn, reviewed Sarah's file and x-rays. They all responded in nearly the same language, all giving a similar diagnosis. All stated the blindness would be permanent. Jim Adams read each one intently, hoping for some clue to help Sarah. He found none.

Bill and Marge were glad to have their little girl home again. They both knew life would be so much different for Sarah and for themselves. Nearly all of their savings went towards Sarah's medical expenses, so they were unable to afford the special schooling Sarah needed. Marge searched and was able to obtain books in Braille from the University of Illinois at Urbana. Her friend, Kathy, was a professor there and guided Marge in selecting books and materials she needed to continue Sarah's education at home.

Sarah learned her lessons well, learning Braille in no time at all. Marge would read to Sarah from normal textbooks and once a week a teacher from the local school would give Sarah oral quizzes and tests. The teacher was impressed by Sarah's learning abilities as well as Marge's dedication to teaching

Sarah. Even though Sarah did not physically attend her assigned school, she was the top student in her class. This said a lot about both Sarah and Marge. Marge worked closely with the teachers, principal, and the school board to ensure her daughter's continued enrollment and education.

Sarah also rapidly learned to navigate through the house without bumping into everything. Marge taught her to count steps to wherever she wanted to go and to always keep track of where she was in the house. Bill fashioned a small white stick for Sarah to sweep in front of her to avoid obstacles in the house. Sarah took her blindness well, accepting it and dealing with it. She was a little girl, but she was determined to overcome her handicap.

During this time, I was notified that Caretakers had been dispatched to assist Sarah. The transmissions I made were reviewed by the Caretaker Counsel. This Counsel is a group consisting of both New World and Pre-Life souls. When the Caretaker Counsel finds a Chosen in need of help or comfort, they dispatch a Caretaker. Caretakers are given special power by The Fathers to accomplish their mission. They are able to transfer energy, warmth, and strength to a Chosen. This process was known to me but I did not yet understand it fully.

A Caretakers mission is to provide extra comfort to a Chosen in trouble, ease pain and sorrow, and transfer needed strength. Sarah was in trouble because her blindness and the Counsel decided she needed the aid of a Caretaker. The Caretaker counsel sent two Caretakers to aid Sarah. They both would stay and emit strength to Sarah during her time of need. I really didn't need the notification of their arrival as I immediately felt the warmth, comfort, and strength emitted by them towards Sarah. Bill and Marge were also provided with a Caretaker to assist each of them in coping with the tragedy that befell them.

On many occasions, the Caretaker sent is a close friend or family member of a Chosen. Members of the Caretaker Counsel evaluate the situation and the needs of the Chosen. When it is deemed necessary, the Counsel will contact a close relative of a Chosen residing in the New World and request their assistance. This was true in Sarah's case. One of the Caretakers sent to help Sarah in her time of need was her great-grandmother, Nanna. Bill and Marge were assigned Caretakers at random.

Sarah's speed in learning and adapting was a direct result of Nanna's presence. Nanna's love for Sarah enhanced her transfer of comfort and strength. Even I could feel the love pouring from Nanna to Sarah. Bill and Marge's Caretakers helped them to accept the situation and also directed Marge in her quest to provide the best education as possible for Sarah. They both gained strength and were assisted in coping with Sarah's blindness.

Over time, Sarah's other senses sharpened. She was able to hear vehicles approaching the farm long before they ever turned into the lane. She was also able to smell and taste the air, predicting forthcoming weather. Bill and Marge had expected part of this enhancement of Sarah's senses. They were told that her other senses would help compensate for her loss of sight. What they didn't know was the level to which her remaining senses would grow.

Too Much Snow

Just after the time of Sarah's first full year of blindness, she began displaying uncanny predictions of weather. The first was near Thanksgiving. Bill and Marge were making plans to visit his parents in Northern Indiana. Sarah sat at the dining room table, listening to the conversation. Bill had just told Marge the route they would take and his approximation of how long it would take to get there.

Suddenly, Sarah sat completely upright, her unseeing eyes staring forward. Marge noticed Sarah's sudden change in posture and asked, "What is it, Sarah?" Sarah nervously said, "Daddy, we can't go that way." "There is too much snow." "Do we have to go?" Bill leaned back in his chair, looking at Sarah. The look of fear on her face concerned him. He thought for a moment, considering what Sarah had just said.

"Sarah, there isn't much snow this time of year." Bill finally replied. Sarah still sat erect, gazing forward. "Yes, daddy." "Lots of snow, too much snow." Sarah responded. She continued, "We can't go that way, daddy." "There is too much snow!" Bill contemplated for a minute, then said, "We could go to Indianapolis and then go North from there." "The roads are a bit better and we might make better time too." Sarah said happily, "Yes, much better." and relaxed in her chair.

Bill and Marge looked at one another dumbfounded. "Well, it's settled then." "We go by way of Indianapolis." Bill said, not really knowing why. Sarah sighed what seemed a sigh of relief and whispered, "Good."

The Robinsons loaded the truck early in the morning, the day before Thanksgiving. Bill wanted to get an early start in order to arrive at his parents farm by early afternoon. The sky was gray as Bill hurried Marge and Sarah out of the house and into the truck. A light snow started falling as he left the farmhouse lane. Within an hour they left the snow behind them and Sarah fell peacefully asleep. It wasn't long until Marge nodded off also.

As Bill had expected, he turned the truck into his parents farm in the early afternoon. He thought aloud many times that the light snow he had been driving through for the past couple of hours would cause a greater delay. He reached over, nudged Marge and Sarah, and said. "Wake up, you two." "We're here."

Marge opened her eyes and got her bearings in a matter of seconds. She could see the farmhouse and said, "So we are." "Sarah, grandpa is on the porch waiting for us." "Wake up, honey." George Robinson, Bill's father, began waving to them and yelled toward the house, "Martha, they're here!"

George reached the truck as soon as Bill had stopped. He opened the passenger door and told Marge, "You two go on in the house." "Bill and I will get your things from the back." Marge and Sarah climbed out of the truck and headed toward the house as Bill and George began unloading luggage. George called out to Bill, "Better hurry, son." "There's a storm coming." Bill and George quickly grabbed everything from the back of the truck and carried them to the house.

Once inside, George told Bill, "We were afraid you had gotten trapped in the storm." "I just heard on the radio that many people are getting stranded between Kankakee and the Indiana border." "We know you always come that way." "But, it looks like you made it through all right."

Bill looked at Marge and said, "We didn't come that way, dad." "We went across to Indianapolis and then straight up to here." Marge said, "That's right." "Sarah told us there would be a lot of snow the other way." Marge looked at Bill and said, with a catch in her voice, "We would have gotten stranded if it weren't for Sarah."

Bill explained to his parents how Sarah predicted the storm and how he had changed his traveling plans. Marge gave Sarah a strong hug, said "Stay in here, Sarah." and followed the others into the kitchen. Sarah searched through the pile of luggage and found her suitcase. She easily found it because of the raised "S" Marge had attached to the side. She opened it, took out a book, and sat down. She ran her fingers across the pages and began reading where she had left off.

I watched Sarah and began thinking about what had just happened. Sarah had somehow predicted the snowstorm and guided her family safely. As I ran the question through my mind, I could hear the same question being repeated in the kitchen, "How could she possibly know there would be a severe snowstorm?"

A minute later George approached Sarah, the others closely following him. Sarah cocked her head, as if listening, and said, "Hi grandpa." She carefully laid her book aside and stood up. She stretched out her arms as a signal and George bent down and gave her a hug. George asked, "Sarah, how did you know about the snowstorm?" A puzzled look came across Sarah's face and she replied, "I don't know." "I just tasted it." George now had a puzzled look and asked, "Tasted it?" He looked at Bill and Marge questioningly. Before they could reply, Sarah said, "Yes, and it tasted like a lot." Not knowing what else to say, George shrugged and dropped the subject by saying, "Well, it doesn't matter." "What matters is that all three of you are safely here." Sarah reached out her arms toward her grandmother and Martha responded by giving Sarah a hug and a kiss on the cheek. The adults wandered back to the kitchen and Sarah picked up her book and resumed her reading.

The Thanksgiving weekend passed without any further mention of what Sarah had done. At least there was no further mention within the Robinson household. However, the history I was recording and transmitting did attract the attention of the Caretakers and the Watchers. The Watchers are interested in any unusual events that are recorded and the prediction Sarah had made caught their attention. Both Counsels were concerned that Sarah's prediction may, in some way, be related to the presence of Sarah's Caretakers.

Caretakers have the ability to provide comfort and

strength to a Chosen, but are forbidden from influencing events, as are all New World travelers. Nanna's actions, as well as Simone's, Sarah's other Caretaker, were evaluated by both Counsels. All records were thoroughly reviewed, but no influence over Sarah could be found. After the review, members from both Counsels conferred and decided to assign a Watcher to Sarah. Nanna was to remain Sarah's Caretaker, but they felt Simone's presence was no longer required. The Caretaker Counsel re-evaluated Sarah's need and decided it could be handled by Nanna alone. Simone was called back to the New World. The Watcher Counsel assigned Watcher David to watch over and evaluate any further predictions Sarah may make.

More predictions were made by Sarah in the following months. Bill began to take Sarah's weather comments and incorporate them into his daily routine. Each day he would ask her, "What's it taste like today, Sarah?" Sarah's response varied with the weather. Most of the time she would simply say, "Tastes real good, daddy." Bill would then know it would be a nice day. Watcher David analyzed every event to ensure that Caretaker Nanna was not the cause of Sarah's predictions.

As a test, Nanna was recalled to the New World for about a week. Sarah's predictions continued, but she became quiet and sullen. She kept telling Bill and Marge, "I hate being blind." "Why do I have to be blind?" "It would have been better to have died." It was apparent that Sarah needed a Caretakers strength. The test proved there was no influence on Sarah's special abilities by Nanna. Nanna was transported back immediately. Sarah once again gained strength from Nanna and was able to cope with her blindness.

Stormy Darkness

Bill continued to use Sarah's comments to determine the weather and worked the farm according to her predictions. One morning in mid-April, Bill asked Sarah the usual, "What's it taste like today, Sarah?" On this morning, Sarah's reply caused Bill great concern. She answered, "Oh, Daddy, it tastes awful." "How awful?", Bill asked. Sarah continued, "Daddy, I taste a terrible storm." "It tastes like a lot of wind and rain." "Daddy, it makes me want to hide."

Bill didn't have to dwell on Sarah's comments for very long. He immediately knew what she meant and quickly began preparations for the storm that Sarah "tasted". The animals were his first task. By late morning, he had rounded up all the animals and made them as safe as he could. He secured and stored all the farm equipment and made sure the barn and outbuildings were made as storm proof as possible. Then he made sure the house was prepared for the storm.

During this time, Marge was also making preparations.

She made sure there were provisions in the storm cellar. She filled three large milk cans with water and cooked all the perishable foods. All of this she stored in the storm cellar along with as many canned goods as she could. Sarah helped her mother as best she could and even took all of her books to the cellar.

The storm cellar was built by settlers, nearly 100 years previously. It was partially underground and stood like a mound between the house and barn. The door was solid and faced to the Northeast, away from the path of storms. By late afternoon, all preparations had been made. The sky had turned very dark, nearly as dark as night. Bill made last minute checks of everything as Marge and Sarah entered the cellar. He entered a few minutes later and secured the heavy door. He turned to Marge and Sarah and said, "That's about all we can do." "Let's eat!"

The rain started falling as they began eating the fried chicken that Marge had prepared earlier. The wind could be heard howling and whistling outside. Sarah asked, "What's that scratching sound?" Bill listened for a few seconds and then said, "It sounds like a tree limb scratching against the door." He walked to the door and listened further, trying to hear the scratching above the noise of the wind. Suddenly, Sarah yelled, "Dad, it's Suzie!" "Let her in!" Bill unlocked the door and opened it slightly, holding it against the wind. He looked down and saw the yellow puppy entering between his feet. He quickly closed and locked the door after seeing the puppy enter.

Sarah called to her puppy, "Here, Suzie." "Come here, girl." The puppy trotted over to Sarah and shook off the rain, getting Sarah wet in the process. Sarah giggled and said,

"Oh, Suzie." Marge found a towel to dry Sarah and Suzie. As she dried them, she looked at Bill and mouthed the question, "How did she know it was Suzie?" Bill just shrugged his shoulders and shook his head. He had no idea.

I no longer took note of Sarah's predictions and sensing events because I knew Watcher David was keeping track and reporting all events such as this. However, I still wondered about Sarah's special abilities. Was it only because her other senses were sharpened because of her blindness or was there more to it than that? I was also sure Watcher David and the Watcher Counsel were wondering the same thing.

It wasn't long after they had finished eating that Sarah fell asleep, holding Suzie. Bill and Marge quietly discussed the days events as the storm continued above them. "She hit the nail on the head with this one." Bill remarked. "I know, it's amazing." said Marge. "This all can't be just because of her blindness." "There's more to it than that." "Our daughter is a remarkable human being." came Bill's reply. They continued their conversation until they both decided they could not figure how Sarah could know about things in advance. They finally just gave up on the subject and laid down to sleep. They all slept peacefully while the storm continued to rage outside.

Bill was the first to awaken the next morning. Quietly, he left the storm cellar to check any damage to his farm. Marge woke up shortly after Bill had left. She noticed he was gone and could tell he had gone outside because the door was left open. She was checking on Sarah when Bill returned.

Bill had only been gone about 15 minutes, but that had been enough time for him to determine damage caused by the storm. Marge turned as she heard him enter. His face was solemn and Marge asked, "What is it Bill?" Bill related to her that the barn was intact and the animals were all safe. He told her that there was minor damage to some of the outbuildings and that all the farm equipment appeared to be undamaged. Then he became quiet for a moment and held Marge by the shoulders. Tears swelled in his eyes as he told her, "But, the house, Marge." "The house is gone." He pulled her into him as she began to cry.

The Robinsons stood amongst the rubble that had been their home. Their belongings were strewn along the path of the tornado that had destroyed the house. They appeared as if their whole lives had been destroyed in one swoop. I knew it was hard for them as they began to salvage what precious memories they could. Marge found one of Sarah's old baby pictures and fell to her knees crying, "Why, oh why has this happened?" Sarah heard her mother and went to her, picking her way through the debris. She found her, wrapped her arms around her mother, and said, "It's ok, Mom." "Jackie will help us."

I was shocked. "Jackie?" I thought. Sarah knew no one by that name. The only Jackie was Marge's Caretaker. I imagined Watcher David was thinking the same thing I was, "How does she know about Jackie?"

Marge turned on one knee to Sarah and asked, "Who, Sarah?" Sarah repeated, "It's ok, Mom." "Jackie will help us." Marge asked, "Who's Jackie, Sarah?" Sarah replied, "The angel that helps you, Mom." "Daddy has one too, her name is Samantha." Marge had a look of disbelief as she said, "Sarah, what are you talking about?" Sarah gazed to the right and lifted her head and said, "There, mommy." "Jackie is right there." Marge followed Sarah's gaze and said, "There's no one there, Sarah." Apparently, Jackie moved off a distance as Sarah replied, "She's gone now."

I could hardly believe what had just happened. Not only did Sarah know the names of the Caretakers, she had pointed Jackie out to Marge. I could only imagine what Watcher David and Caretaker Jackie were thinking. I was sure the Counsels were buzzing with activity at this sensing event.

I later discovered that the Counsels were indeed excited. Watcher David as well as all Caretakers were immediately recalled to the New World. All records were once again scrutinized and Nanna, Jackie, Samantha, and David were all questioned at length. But, in the meantime, the Robinsons were having a difficult time.

Marge began accusing Bill of allowing the house to be destroyed. She wasn't able to cope with the loss and also ignored Sarah. Bill became despondent and kept talking to himself, "Why didn't I do more?" "It's my fault the house and everything we had is gone." Sarah was much worse off. Her parents were like strangers to her. They would argue and tell her, "Go away, Sarah." "Just go to your room." I would follow as she sobbed her way to her room. It all was made worse as they were in a strange house. Sarah had a difficult time finding her way. She would stumble into things and fall on many occasions. Her ninth birthday came a few days after the horrible storm. That day passed unnoticed by Bill and Marge. Sarah commented to herself that she was no longer loved or needed, "They don't care about me anymore." "They don't love me." Every night she would cry herself to sleep, no one to tuck her into bed. My heart was breaking for this sweet little girl.

I took note of all these things and filed a special report. I was fearful that the Anti-Savers would take advantage of the Robinson's current situation. I knew it wouldn't take much for the darkness of an Anti-Saver to enter and consume their lives. The Anti-Savers and their darkness are a powerful and evil force.

The Searcher Counsel advised me that things were still being investigated by the Caretaker and Watcher Counsels. All I could do was observe, record, report, and pray the Anti-Savers would not have time to adversely influence the Robinsons.

May 1, 1964 became the turning point for the Robinsons. The day started with Bill and Marge arguing at the breakfast table. Sarah soon began crying and yelled, "Stop it!" "STOP IT!" She took her little white stick and began waving it across the table, upsetting glasses and plates. Bill grabbed at the stick until he caught it in his hand. He jerked the stick from Sarah's hand, causing her to be pulled up onto the kitchen table. I was horrified at what happened next and found myself yelling, "NO!"

My worst fear had suddenly become reality. Darkness from an unknown Anti-Saver had entered. I immediately sent notification to the Counsel, but was once again told the investigation was not yet completed. My mind was full of helplessness as I watched.

Bill lifted the white stick and with what appeared all his strength, beat Sarah across the back. Again and again he lifted the stick and struck Sarah. Marge yelled, "Bill, stop!" "STOP!" Bill then swung the stick and struck Marge across the face, sending her to the floor. As she fell with a heavy thud, Bill realized what he had done. Shaking uncontrollably, he dropped the stick and ran out the back door, stopping to throw up. The next thing I heard was the truck starting and gravel being thrown as Bill sped down the lane.

Marge lay unconscious on the floor, a bleeding gash across her cheek. Sarah was lying across the table, the back of her light blue dress ripped and darkening from blood oozing from the wounds in her back. Tears came to my eyes as I saw Sarah lying there. I was totally helpless and could only wait and see what would happen next.

About ten minutes after Bill left, I heard a police car and ambulance approaching the house. As it pulled up, I saw Bill sitting in the back seat of the police car, crying and trembling. The emergency technicians examined Marge and Sarah and transported them to the hospital. Bill was taken to jail.

The following day, Marge and Sarah were released from the hospital and returned to the house. The Caretakers and Watcher David were finally reassigned. Bill was released two days later when Marge refused to file assault charges. Things improved dramatically once the Caretakers were back. The Anti-Saver's darkness was pushed aside by the Caretakers and I knew things would be all right. Bill and Marge realized that the storm and the loss of the house was an accident. They reconciled with one another and Marge forgave Bill's outburst. Deep within her, she knew it wasn't his fault. They once again showed love and affection to one another and to Sarah. Belatedly, Sarah's birthday was celebrated and they became a family again. They rebuilt their house and moved back to their own farm in time to celebrate Christmas.

The Caretaker and Watcher Counsels allowed the return

of the Caretakers under certain conditions. Since Sarah had lost sense of Jackie when Jackie moved back a few feet, it was decided that no one, including myself, was to ever come closer than six feet to Sarah, if at all possible. The Counsels advised The Fathers of their decision and had full approval from them. The missions would continue.

Sarah still made her predictions, but no longer talked about the presence of angels. It seemed the comment Sarah had made to Marge the day after the storm was completely forgotten. Time passed by unnoticed for another 9 years. Sarah's 18th birthday came and went and her graduation from high school was over. Another Summer was beginning.

Daniel and Donald

Sarah applied and was accepted to attend college at the University of Illinois. Her dream was to become a child psychologist. She commented to her parents, "I want to make a difference in children's lives somehow." Marge told her, "You can become anything, Sarah." "Set your mind to what you want and you will get there." The whole summer was spent preparing Sarah for college. She and Marge visited the campus nearly every day and mapped out Sarah's course from one building to another. They were granted permission to enter the buildings and classrooms where Sarah's classes would be held. By summers end, Sarah knew her way all around campus.

Sarah continued to live at home and Marge would drive her to and from school. It was difficult for Sarah as most textbooks were not available in Braille. Marge assisted in reading to her and Sarah would use a small tape recorder for lectures and to keep notes. I knew Nanna and the other

Caretakers were hard at work as Sarah soon progressed to the top of her class.

One day while Sarah was walking to her final class of the day, some students rushed into her and knocked her down. They continued about their way without regard to her. Sarah became confused and forgot her position. A scared look came over her face and it appeared she was about to panic. "Nanna, help me." she whispered. Her professor from her previous class had seen the crowd push Sarah aside and was now approaching her. He asked, "Sarah, are you all right?" Sarah turned in his direction and responded, "I've lost my count and don't know how to get to my next class." "Could you please help me, Professor Gray?"

Donald Gray was a psychology professor and had lost his right arm and right eye in battle in Vietnam. He also assisted other veterans in overcoming their own physical losses. He placed his briefcase on the grass, reached out his left hand and said, "Here, take my hand." Sarah reached out and waved her arm until she felt his arm. He grasped her hand and helped her to her feet. He then picked up her cane and handed it to her. He retrieved his briefcase and walked Sarah to her next class.

I briefly contemplated why Sarah asked for Nanna's help. Was she just afraid and calling to her great-grandmother for help? Did she know Nanna was close by? I knew David was evaluating the event and quickly dismissed the incident.

Sarah told her mother what happened that day and how Professor Gray had assisted her. Sarah said, "I think he is a very nice man." "What do you think, Mom?" Marge replied, "Why, Sarah." "It sounds like you have a crush on Professor

Gray." Sarah just gazed forward and said, "No, mother." "I love Daniel."

I nearly jumped out of my New Life skin! Daniel? She couldn't mean me. I went over everyone Sarah knew and there were only two other Daniels she remotely knew. One was her cousin in Indiana. The other was a student in her psychology class and she didn't know him very well at all. She did mean me! My heart and mind were racing.

Marge looked at Sarah and asked, "Daniel?" "Who's Daniel?" Sarah appeared to think for a moment and replied with a smile, "Just someone close to me I have known for a very long time." Marge glanced at Sarah as she drove, as if trying to figure out who Sarah was talking about. When they arrived at the farm, Marge stopped and shut off the car. She turned to Sarah and said, "Sarah, I don't know a Daniel close to you." "Who is this boy you are in love with?" Sarah replied a bit angrily, "Mother, it isn't a boy!" "He's a man!"

Marge sat in the car, her mouth open. She appeared as if she were in shock. After a moment or so she finally spoke, "A man?" "What man?" "I don't know of a man named Daniel." Marge became frustrated as she continued, "Sarah, you don't know any men." "How could you know a man?" "Just who is this Daniel?" "Sarah, answer me!"

My mind was running full blast. I was asking myself similar questions and others such as, "How could she know about me?" "She can't possibly mean me!" "If not me, then who is Sarah talking about?" I also began wondering what must be going through Watcher David's mind and what he was reporting to the Counsel. THE COUNSEL! Now I really began to think hard. "What would the Counsel think?"

"What would they do?" A dozen possibilities came to mind. The most obvious was that they would remove me from the mission and from Sarah. I then thought of what might happen if I were recalled to the New World. I wondered if someone else would replace me or if the mission would be ended, stranding Sarah. That final possibility really frightened me. I thought, "They would never do that, would they?" I was nearly at my wits end when Sarah's giggling drew me away from my thoughts.

Sarah giggled and said, "Oh, mother!" "You should hear yourself." "There is no Daniel." She began laughing aloud. Marge replied, "Sarah, you Imp!" "You nearly gave me heart failure!" Sarah continued laughing and said, "I'm sorry, mother." "But you should have heard yourself." "I just couldn't resist teasing you." Her continued laughter made Marge laugh also. "It is pretty funny at that." she said. Both were laughing so hard that tears came to their eyes. After a few minutes the laughter died down and they dried their eyes. Marge then said, "Well, just don't ever do that to me again." Sarah giggled and whispered, "Don't worry, I won't."

A great relief came over me. I assumed that the same happened with Watcher David and the Counsel. The incident must have been dismissed as a joke on Marge as I heard nothing from the Searcher Counsel. I was once again happy knowing I would remain with Sarah.

As they left the car and were walking to the house, Sarah paused. She turned around and appeared to be looking directly at me. She touched her lips briefly and then placed her hand over her heart. This action dumbfounded me. I couldn't figure out why she had done that. I thought she was saying some sort of prayer because she lowered her head as she touched her heart. I watched her turn and follow Marge into the house. I followed them both, making sure I kept my distance.

The days and nights continued as before. Over the next few months however, Sarah quit making weather predictions for her father. When Bill would ask about the weather, Sarah would simply reply, "I don't know, daddy." "I just don't taste anything anymore." Bill soon stopped asking her altogether. Bill commented to Marge, "Guess she's grown out of it."

It was at this time that Marge related to Bill about how Sarah reacted when she asked her about having a crush on Professor Gray. Bill's eyes widened as he said, "She's in love with Professor Gray." "Well, I'll be." "No wonder she isn't interested in the weather." He continued, "Now things are beginning to make sense." "That's why she wants to work with him this summer."

Sarah had done quite well in her studies and Professor Gray had recommended Sarah for a position at his clinic. He had many veterans he worked with as well as children that required special help. When Sarah was offered the chance to work with children, she immediately accepted the position. She remarked to her parents, "This is going to be a great summer!"

Sarah spent many hours with Professor Gray and the children during the following months of summer. Sarah seemed to enjoy working with him and even got in the habit of calling him Donald. He had insisted on that as he didn't feel comfortable being called Professor Gray at the clinic. Sarah remained busy, helping the children all that she could. She had a natural way of making the children at ease. The children began referring to her as Angel Sarah.

Sarah shared her love and strength with the children by telling them stories about angels. She told them how each person has their own guardian angel to watch over them. Sarah explained to them that angels were everywhere and all someone had to do was ask for help and the angels would help them. Each day the stories would keep the children wide-eyed with wonder. The children appeared to be coping with their own problems much better because of Sarah and her stories. Many times, the adults would stay and listen to Sarah while waiting to see Professor Gray.

My Angels

The summer passed quickly and the new semester was about to begin. Sarah seemed a bit sad on her last day at the clinic. One of the children noticed this and asked her, "Angel Sarah, why are you sad?" Sarah answered, "Today is my last day working here." "I start my classes again next week." "I'm going to miss all of you so much." Another child then asked, "Can't you take classes and help us too, Angel Sarah?" Sarah looked as if she were about to cry when from the doorway came, "Of course she can." "If she really wants to." It was Donald, entering the room. He approached Sarah and the children. He continued, "Maybe we can get Angel Sarah to visit on Saturdays." "How about it, Sarah?" "Want the job?" Sarah's voice sparkled as she responded, "Of course I do!" The children became excited and were saying, "Angel Sarah isn't leaving!" "Hooray!"

Listening to Sarah's stories brought back memories of my own Pre-Life childhood. When I was a child, I thought my uncle was my guardian angel. He had died when I was young and his death seemed to have affected me in some way. I now knew that he wasn't my guardian angel. He wasn't even in the New World yet. He died many years before I did, but I arrived in the New World before him. To date, the random selection process had only chosen me and one of my sisters. The other members of my family have yet to be chosen. This was true even in Sarah's case. Her death was over 40 years prior to my own, yet here I was recording her life for her ReBirth. That meant that about 85 years will have passed for me at the time of Sarah's death. Time is a strange thing.

Reflecting about angels, especially guardian angels made me think of my Saver and Guide, Robert. I imagined that a Saver could be thought of as a sort of guardian. We watched over Pre-Life souls and brought them back to the New World. We guided them in the New World, helping them understand and teaching them new ways. A Chosen becomes a part of each Saver, mainly because the Saver has been with them every step of the way from birth and death in the Old World to their ReBirth and understanding of the New World.

I was taken away from my thoughts as Sarah's day at the clinic ended. Donald walked Sarah to where Marge was waiting. As they strolled along, he asked if she would join him for supper to celebrate her continued involvement at the clinic. Sarah replied, "That would be wonderful, Donald." "But, I have a better idea." "You come to my house instead." "How about it?" Donald agreed and suggested Sarah ask her mother if it was all right. Sarah spoke to Marge briefly and called out to him, "Be there at 7." He approached the car and verified that it was all right with Marge. She told him, "You are welcome anytime." He quietly replied, "Thank you, Mrs.

Robinson." "I'll be there at 7."

Donald followed the car with his eyes as they drove away. Inside, Marge said, "So, it's Donald now." Sarah cocked her head in Marge's direction and replied, "Oh, Mother!" "Don't be getting any ideas." She then giggled to herself.

The dinner went well, with Donald complimenting both Marge and Sarah. Donald wanted to help with the dishes afterwards, but Marge told Sarah to entertain him on the front porch. Sarah lead Donald to the porch swing. They sat, swinging, talking about the clinic until it was time for Donald to leave. He once again thanked Marge for the wonderful dinner and gave Sarah a hug. "See you next Saturday, Sarah." "And don't be late." he added jokingly.

Sarah began classes the following week and worked at the clinic every Saturday. She talked to Donald both on campus and at the clinic. Things seemed to be going very well between them. He continued to be invited for dinner as well as taking Sarah out to eat once in awhile. They both exchanged gifts at Christmas and Donald surprised Sarah with his birthday gift to her.

It was April 17, 1975, Sarah's 20th birthday. Sarah's parents invited a few people to the party, including Donald Gray. The party was small, but very nice and everyone enjoyed themselves. Just when the last guest had left, Donald took Sarah by the hand and said, "Sarah, come walk with me." They walked and talked for a few minutes until Donald stopped near the old storm cellar. Donald remarked how beautiful the sunset was, trying to describe it to Sarah. He had just finished telling her the colors he saw when he said, "Sarah. the sunset doesn't compare to your beauty." "I love you, Sarah." "I want you to become my wife." "Will you marry me?"

Sarah's eyebrows raised as she heard Donald's question. She thought for a moment before responding, "Donald, I don't want to hurt you, but I can't marry you." Donald asked, "Can't marry me?" "Why not?" Sarah tried explaining that she did not feel the same toward him as he did her. She expressed sorrow for making him think that she was also in love with him. He reassured her that it wasn't her fault.

As Donald left that evening, Sarah whispered to him, "Donald, I'm sorry." Then I heard her say something else, but her lips did not move. No one else seemed to hear her even though it seemed loud and clear. She said, "Daniel." It appeared I was the only one that heard Sarah. Days went by and there was nothing about the incident from the Counsel. I dismissed the incident, thinking it was just my imagination.

The Saturday following Sarah's birthday, she related a story to the children that included special angels that do nothing but watch over them. She told the children these angels were there to help them get to heaven. The story she told was beautiful.

Sarah sat in front of the children and related this story: Once upon a time, an Angel came from heaven to watch over a little girl. The Angel had no special powers to heal the little girl when she would get hurt. The only power this Angel had was to care about the little girl so she could go to heaven. The Angel loved the little girl very much, even though the Angel could not tell her. The Angel watched over the little girl every second, night and day. She tried to talk to the Angel but the Angel couldn't hear her. Other people didn't understand why she was trying to talk to the Angel. So, she tried to talk to the Angel with her mind. She tried every night when she went to sleep. She would fall asleep thinking and trying to talk to the Angel with her mind. Then one day when she was older, the Angel finally heard her. The little girl was now a woman. She talked to the Angel and knew the Angel loved her very much. The Angel walked with her and they talked with their minds. Not long after this she became sick. The Angel had no powers to help her. She knew her time to leave this world was near. She died peacefully and walked with her Angel into heaven. The Angel welcomed her into heaven and taught her love and peace. Now she walks through heaven with her Angel.

Donald was standing at the doorway listening to Sarah's story. He watched the children as they sat and listened. He could see the wonder in their eyes, just as I could. The day ended with Sarah's story and it was time for the children to leave. Donald helped Sarah put some books away and asked, "Sarah, how do you come up with all of these Angel stories?" Sarah replied, "They just come to me." "Amazing." said Donald. "Would you mind if I recorded your stories when you tell them?" he asked. "I don't mind." she said. Donald then explained to her that he wanted to put her stories in writing and maybe create a book of her Angel stories. Sarah thought that was a great idea. She said, "With my stories in a book, so many other children would be able to read them." "That is a great idea, Donald." she said as she gave him a hug.

Each Saturday, Donald would set up the tape recorder and start the machine when Sarah began her stories. By the end of summer, all of Sarah's stories and been recorded. Donald told Sarah he was having his secretary transcribe the stories from the tapes and that he had sent a sample of them to an Army friend that was now a publisher.

He related to Sarah that his friend was with him when he was injured. John Wilson owed his life to Donald Gray. Donald had saved John's life and lost his right arm and eye in the process. Donald told Sarah that one day while on patrol in the jungle, John stepped on a land mine. The mine didn't explode and both men knew that the mine would explode if John moved. Donald dug around the mine in an attempt to disarm it. He was unable to disarm the mine, so he slipped his knife into the trigger to hold it and stepped back. He then pushed John off the mine as hard as he could. The mine exploded a half second later. Donald shielded John, receiving shrapnel in his arm and face in the process.

"I'm sure he will publish your stories." "Not because of our friendship, but because they are such wonderful stories." Donald told her after he related how he had saved John's life. Sarah said, "That would be so wonderful, Donald." "Oh, and don't forget." "We must also have them published in Braille." Sarah was so excited about the possibility of having her stories made into a book that she kissed Donald on the cheek.

That night Sarah told her parents about her stories and how they might be published. With the excitement of starting her third year of school and a possible book, Sarah took a long time to fall asleep that night. I watched her toss and turn until she finally lay still. A few moments later I thought I heard, "Isn't it all so wonderful?" It was Sarah's voice, but she was fast asleep and couldn't have said anything. I figured it was an echo in my mind of what she had said to her parents before coming to bed. I began to wonder if my excitement for Sarah was affecting my imagination. I laughed to myself and promptly dismissed the thought.

The following Saturday, a man briefly interrupted Sarah's session with the children as he attempted to silently close the door. Sarah said, "Come in and sit with us." He found a place to sit near the back of the small room. Sarah continued her session by asking the children, "Who can tell me why it is important to like yourself?" A small girl answered, "If you don't like yourself, you can't really like someone else." Sarah said, "Very good, Cindy." Sarah then went child by child, having them tell what they most liked about themselves and why. Each response was different and unique for each child.

Sarah then ended the session for the day and dismissed the children. As usual, each child stopped to give Sarah a hug before they left. The man approached Sarah as the last child left the room. "Sarah, my name is John Wilson." he said and held out his hand. Sarah waved her hand briefly and found his hand. As she shook his hand she said, "Mr. Wilson, what a nice surprise." "Donald has told me a lot about you." John led Sarah to a chair and asked her to sit down. He then pulled up a chair and sat facing her. "Sarah, you are great with the children." he said. "Why, thank you." she replied. John Wilson then told her about how much he enjoyed reading her stories. "They are simple, yet very beautiful." he said. He continued by telling her that he wanted to publish them. He said he would need her help in arranging the stories the way she wanted them to appear in the book.

All during the time John Wilson was commenting on her stories, Sarah was smiling happily. When she heard that her stories were going to be made into a book that she would help arrange, she could hardly sit still. John's final remark, "And here is a check for five thousand dollars as an advance."

caused Sarah to stand and say, "I can't believe it!" "This is so exciting!" She located John, gave him a hug, kissed his cheek and said, "Oh, thank you so much." "This is more than I could have dreamed of." "I must tell Donald." John took Sarah by the arm and they went to find Donald.

When he heard the news, Donald Gray seemed more excited than Sarah. "This is just fantastic!" "Sarah, I'm so happy for you." he said as he picked her up with his one arm and squeezed her tight. He carefully put her down and exclaimed, "Let's celebrate!"

Sarah's book, titled "MY ANGELS", was published and in bookstores by December first. The bookstores were quickly sold out and many orders were coming in for more. John Wilson told all of this to Sarah and Donald as he presented Sarah with her first royalty check. John told Sarah, "I knew it was a good book, but even I never dreamed it would be like this." He went on to tell her that the bookstores were ordering faster than the printer could keep up with. "This is going to be the next best-seller!" he exclaimed.

Sure enough, "MY ANGELS", became a best selling book. It remained that way for a very long time. Over time, it was published not only in Braille, but in over 100 languages as well. By the time Sarah was 21, she was becoming a very wealthy young lady.

Nancy

The summer after Sarah's 21st birthday saw many changes in her life. She was rapidly becoming known around the world as the author of "MY ANGELS". Sarah visited many cities around the country to speak to groups about her life and to tell her angel stories. People continually praised her and she spent many hours autographing copies of the book for them. She received money for her appearances, even though she didn't want people paying to see her.

From the money she was earning from book sales and her appearances, Sarah created a foundation to help provide for children. She named it the Angel Nanna Foundation in memory of her great-grandmother. The first accomplishment of the foundation was to build a school for handicapped children. The goal of the school was to help children accept their condition and become successful despite any limitations. Many such schools would be built in the years to come.

The summer passed quickly and Sarah was asked to tour

not only the country, but also the world. Sarah declined. Instead, she wanted to finish her education. She also wanted to spend time helping children at Professor Gray's clinic. She told Donald and John, "I must finish my education." "I want to learn more in order to better help the children." The two men accepted her response and didn't pressure her to go on the tours. "We can wait and do the tours next summer." she said.

So, Sarah returned to school and resumed her work at the clinic. She enjoyed talking to the children and they were comforted by her. She encouraged them to write about their feelings and create their own stories. One of the older girls, Nancy, put her feelings into a poem. Nancy was only 15, but Sarah was touched by a poem Nancy read to her. Sarah sat silently as Nancy read her poem.

Around the world the Angels travel
never tiring of giving their LOVE.
They don't ask for anything from us
as they provide comfort with their LOVE.

Strength is given to all who request
guidance from the bottom of their HEART.
Angels never turn a cold shoulder
to those needing a warm Angel HEART.

A pure heart begins with a pure mind
thinking nearly like that of a CHILD.
The Angels flock to hearts that are pure
and to souls that behave as a CHILD.

Open your heart and allow them in
and seek the warmth and love of ANGELS.
There is no greater love to be found
than that of the children and ANGELS.

Tears came to Sarah's eyes as Nancy read her poem. She dried her eyes when Nancy finished and said, "Nancy, that is very beautiful and touching."

Sarah began spending more and more time with Nancy in the following months. Sarah's heart went out to Nancy. Nancy was a very troubled girl. Nancy's mother had died when she was five years old and her father had sexually abused her most of her life. She loved him and hated him at the same time. She was joyful when he died, but was also tormented by his death. Nancy blamed herself for what her father had done to her. In some way she felt it was her fault. She had related to Sarah her guilt about his death. She had wished for him to stop doing things to her and now her wish was fulfilled. He would never again touch her and Nancy felt it was her fault he was dead. When her father died, she went to live her mother's older sister. Her aunt was the only living relative that Nancy had.

Sarah worked diligently and became very attached to Nancy. She would bring her to the farm as often as she could. It was during one of these visits that bad news came to Nancy and the Robinsons. The visit was prearranged to coincide with a weekend trip Nancy's aunt had planned.

An Illinois State Trooper visited the Robinson farm early in the morning after Nancy's first evening at the farm. Bill answered the door and stepped out onto the front porch to talk to the Trooper. The officer spoke kindly, "Sorry to disturb you sir." "Do you know someone by the name of Barbara Sullivan?" Bill said that he knew her and that her niece was spending the weekend because Barbara was going to visit friends in St. Louis. The officer continued, "Do you know of any other relatives she may have?" Bill replied. "She has no other living relatives."

The Trooper then explained to Bill that Barbara had been killed in an accident about twenty miles from St. Louis. The officers at the scene determined that she must have fallen asleep and lost control of her car as there were no skid marks where the car went off the road. The car had rolled several times, coming to rest in an open field. It was assumed that Barbara had been killed instantly. In searching through her belongings they had found Bill's address. Other information about her family had not been found. The officer explained that he had been sent to Bill's address in an attempt locate a next of kin. The officer gathered what information he could from Bill regarding Barbara and Nancy. He then thanked Bill and departed.

Later that day, a state vehicle arrived at the farm. Two representatives from the Illinois Department of Children and Family Services came for Nancy. Since she was a minor and had no living relatives, Nancy became a state responsibility. However, Nancy didn't want to leave. Sarah talked to her for awhile and convinced her that it would be best to go. She also assured her, "You won't be there long." "We will have you back here in no time."

The next time Nancy saw Sarah was at her aunt's funeral. After the funeral, Bill told Nancy, "Don't worry Nancy, we are working to have you come live with us." "It won't be long." Sarah hugged Nancy and said, "We will be together again soon, Nancy."

It was difficult for Sarah, knowing how alone Nancy was in the world. She discussed Nancy's fate with Marge and Bill. All three had become very attached to Nancy and loved her very much. When Nancy was taken by the state, Bill had called his lawyer to arrange for him and Marge to obtain custody of Nancy. He had asked Marge and Sarah, "Do you want Nancy to live here always?" The answer from both was a resounding "YES!"

Jerry Wilkins, Bills lawyer, came to the house shortly after they returned from Barbara's funeral. "I have very good news, Bill." were his first words. Jerry was excited as he explained how the Robinsons could gain custody of Nancy. He said, "I have the paper work all prepared and a court date is set." "I have also included a petition for adoption as you requested." "We can obtain custody and immediately file for adoption." "We go to court for the custody hearing on next Monday." Bill and Marge were overjoyed at what Jerry had told them. Sarah was very excited and said, "Nancy will be my sister!"

That night, Sarah had difficulty falling asleep and kept saying, "Nancy, my sister." After awhile she lay silent and I heard her say, "Isn't it wonderful?" Without thinking, I heard myself saying, "Yes it is, Sarah." Then I heard Sarah say, "Daniel, you finally heard me?"

I was in a near panic at what I just heard and backed away. Sarah was calling to me, "Daniel?" "Daniel, are you there?" Her voice faded the further I went until I could no longer hear her. It dawned on me that Sarah was speaking to me using telepathy. All the other times I heard her were not just my imagination.

My first thought upon realizing this was to report all of the incidents to the Counsel. I considered the possibilities and consequences of reporting them and knew I would either be called back to the New World and possibly lose Sarah or be told to stay out of her range. I decided it would be best not to report anything and just stay only as close to Sarah as was necessary. It seemed that her communication could only happen when she fell asleep, so I stayed as far back as I could when she would go to bed.

The custody hearing lasted about 30 minutes, resulting in Bill and Marge being awarded custody of Nancy. Jerry filed the adoption petition immediately afterwards and a court date of December 20th was assigned, less than 2 months away. Nancy went home with the Robinsons to begin her new life. Sarah helped Nancy unpack her things and settle into her room. They sat and talked for awhile and Sarah told Nancy that she loved her and that hopefully they would soon be sisters. Before leaving Nancy for the night she told her this brief story:

My Angel does not have wings, but she can fly. My Angel watches over me and cares for my needs. She gives me strength when I am weak and warms my heart when it is cold. My Angel loves me, just as Your Angel loves you. Your Angel is there, helping you and loving you. Open your heart to Your Angel as I have opened my heart to mine. You too can experience the love of an Angel. Angels don't care what you look like, if you have limbs, or eyes that see. They love you as you are, asking for nothing from you. So, give Your Angel your thanks and your love. Do the best you can in everything you do to prove your love to Your Angel. Help others as Your Angel helps you. Love others as Your Angel loves you.

Nancy seemed to enjoy living with the Robinsons, but she still felt somewhat alone. She confessed this to Sarah by saying, "I'm grateful and very happy here, but somehow I feel out of place." "I really don't know what it is besides not having a family anymore." Sarah thought for a moment and said, "I know it's hard for you Nancy, but you do have a family." "We are your family and soon I will be your real sister." "In the meantime, write your feelings in your poetry." "I think it will really help you."

A few days later, Nancy asked Sarah to come to her room after supper. When Sarah entered Nancy's room, Nancy guided her to a chair and said, "I have something I want to read to you." "I thought about what you said about putting my feelings into my poetry." Nancy went to her desk and picked up a sheet of paper. "I hope you like this." she said. Without another word, Nancy began reading.

She was the first one in my sight
after my eyes focused to see.
She gave warmth by holding me tight
and sharing her warm voice with me.

She held me close so I would know
all of the love she had inside.
She guides me wherever I go
and by her rules I will abide.

She wasn't in my life for long
because she was wanted above.
She taught me what was right and wrong
and gave me all of her love.

She is gone but I won't forget
her words and what she gave to me.
She still resides within me yet
to make of me what I should be.

She lived her life better than most
and gave more than any other.
She may not approve of my boast
that she was the worlds best Mother.

When Nancy finished, Sarah said, "That's very moving, Nancy." "It really shows how much you love your mother." "You have a way of expressing yourself through poetry." "I think you have a natural talent." "I hope you continue to write more poems." Nancy gave Sarah a hug and thanked her for being a part of her life.

On December 20, 1976, Bill and Marge were anxious as they entered the courtroom. Jerry told them, "I don't expect any opposition from the State." "Hopefully, this won't take very long." Sarah sat with Jerry and her parents. Nancy was sitting with her appointed lawyer at the next table. They all stood as the judge entered. Then, each side presented their case and their views.

The hearing lasted nearly 40 minutes. Bill and Marge hugged Sarah and each other when the judge announced, "Petition for adoption is hereby granted." Upon hearing this, Nancy immediately stood and ran into Marge's awaiting arms. The Robinson family now had 4 members! The judge didn't appear to mind the interruption as she continued, a big smile on her face, "It is further decreed that Nancy Lee Sims shall be known as Nancy Lee Robinson." "Good luck to all of you." She then closed the proceedings and called for the next case.

Nancy and Sarah sat giggling and hugging one another in the back seat of the car. Each was telling the other about how great it was to have a sister. Both were overjoyed and Nancy said, "Imagine me having a sister and a real mother and father." "I can hardly believe it all." Bill piped up, "Well, believe it daughter." "It's all true." "All our lives are going to be so much better now." Marge added, "Nancy, we are so glad to have you with us." Sarah hugged Nancy close as both shed tears of joy.

That Christmas was the most joyous time I had witnessed with the Robinson family. Having a new member of the family brought on an added dimension. Other relatives came to visit and welcome Nancy as a real family member. Nancy commented to Sarah, "This is overwhelming." "A few weeks ago I had no one." "Now I have so many relatives I don't know what to do!" Sarah just giggled and said, "Even I didn't know I had so many." They both laughed aloud and continued celebrating the day with their family.

By early evening, all the relatives were gone and the four Robinsons were relaxing in the living room. Nancy suddenly said, "Oh, I almost forgot." "I have something for the three of you." She excused herself and went up to her room. She returned a minute later, holding a piece of paper in her hand. She said, "Mom, dad, Sarah, I want to read something, a poem, to you." Sarah said, "Read it Nancy." Bill added, "Yes, please do." Nancy stood silhouetted against the lights of the Christmas tree. She said, "I wrote this after we came back from court, but I saved it until tonight." Nancy then began reading.

My old life is behind me now
as I walk into my new life.
You welcomed me and so I vow
to never cause you grief or strife.

I have a new home and Mother
to comfort, love, and care for me.
I am glad to have another
father who's as nice as can be.

I am grateful for the sister
I have gained as part of the deal.
She is so sweet and I love her
dearly for helping me to heal.

My new life started on this day
because of the gift that you gave.
I became your daughter today
and my life you surely did save.

I love you all so very much
for loving me with all your heart.
This is the first I have known such
love and warmth, let us never part.

There was silence for a moment before Marge started crying and said, "Oh, Nancy." Nancy went to Marge, hugged her, and said, "I love you mom." Marge continued crying and said, "I love you too, Nancy."

The next month passed quickly and soon it was Nancy's birthday. The Robinsons held a small but nice party for her.

A few of Nancy's new friends attended as well as Donald Gray and John Wilson. The day passed quietly and the evening was spent celebrating Nancy's 16th birthday. Near the end of the evening, Nancy called everyone to sit down and opened a notebook. She said, "I have a few poems I would like to read for my friends and family."

Everyone sat quietly as Nancy read poem after poem expressing her feelings about close friends. She also read many more about family and life. Everyone was silent, in awe of what they had just experienced, as she finished reading.

John stood and approached Nancy. "How many poems do you have, Nancy?" he asked. Nancy told him that she must have over a hundred written down. John then asked, "May I read them all?" Nancy answered in the affirmative by nodding her head up and down and said, "Why of course you can Mr. Wilson." She handed him the notebook and he walked to the kitchen, thumbing through the notebook as he went. Everyone else gathered around Nancy, praising her for her poetry.

After Nancy's party was over and her friends had left, the Robinsons and Donald Gray went to the kitchen to see why John was so interested in Nancy's poetry. Donald was the first to speak, "Well John, why so much interest in Nancy's poems?" John answered quietly without looking up from the notebook, "These are good, really good." "Very interesting." John continued his silent reading as everyone else quietly found a seat and waited for John to finish reading. When John finished the last poem he looked up and said to Bill, "Your new daughter is very talented, Bill." He then turned to Nancy and asked. "Nancy, would you mind if I took your notebook with me?" Nancy replied, "I don't mind." "But, why?" John explained that he wanted his secretary to begin typing the poems. He looked at Nancy. "I want to publish these." he said, excitedly waving the notebook in the air. Nancy let out a squeal of delight and asked, "Really?" John said, "Of course I do, these are fantastic!" Sarah cheerfully added, "Another Robinson is about to become famous."

Sarah's words rang true for Nancy. By Sarah's 22nd birthday, "Life, A Collection by Nancy Lee Robinson" was selling very well. Nancy received a small sum every month with the majority of her earnings going to charity and her trust account. The trust would open for her use when she turned 21. Even though Sarah insisted Nancy do other things with her money, Nancy chose to donate half of her book income to her and Sarah's favorite charity, the Angel Nanna Foundation. Nancy told Sarah, "I want to do it." "Besides, someday we both will be involved with the foundation." "We will work together to build schools and help children." Sarah was very pleased with her sister's decision and said, "Yes we will, Nancy."

That summer, Nancy toured with Sarah. They visited many cities throughout the country and even visited a few foreign countries. Sarah and Nancy had a very good time and would always be together wherever they went. Nancy would describe scenery, buildings, and people to Sarah when they had time for sight-seeing. Nancy continued writing poetry and each new place she visited resulted in at least five new poems. Sarah also busied herself by creating new stories. They would quietly sit side by side, Nancy writing poetry and Sarah recording her stories. By the end of the summer, each had enough material for another book. Naturally, both books were immediately published by John Wilson.

Communication

At about this time I started hearing Sarah more clearly at night. I would go as far away as I dared, but her voice was still in my mind. It would only last a minute or so and then fade away. She was trying to make contact with me each time she went to bed. I was unsure as to what to do. I knew I shouldn't answer her calls to me. I debated whether or not to notify the Counsel of what was happening. Each night I would be torn between answering Sarah and remaining silent. Something in the back of my mind told me to report this, but somehow my heart wouldn't let me. Upon realizing that my heart was over ruling what my training indicated, I finally knew that I was in love with Sarah. How it came to be, I don't know. It all seemed like a fog lifting and I knew I must answer Sarah. I waited as long as I could and on Christmas Eve I could no longer bear being silent.

December 24th 1977 was a normal Christmas Eve for the Robinson family. They prepared for Christmas day as any other family would. The Christmas tree was dressed in ornaments and sparkled with twinkling lights. Each family member had placed gifts for one another under the tree and more than once Sarah had picked up one for her and shook it.

She felt for the raised "S" that marked her gifts. When she would find one, she would cock her head and listen intently, making sure she was alone. She would then place the gift close to her ear and shake the package. She looked so sweet and innocent at the foot of the tree, trying to figure out what the package contained. At one point she was listening so intently to the package that she didn't notice Nancy enter the room.

Nancy cleared her throat, "Ahem!" Sarah jumped a bit, startled, and quickly put down the package saying, "Nancy, no fair sneaking up on people." Nancy laughed aloud and said, "Yes, but I did catch you acting like a child." Sarah giggled and replied, "But it's so much fun!" Bill and Marge entered immediately after Nancy and Bill said, "Come on you two, let's get started." Bill, Marge, and Sarah sat on the sofa and Nancy stood outlined by the tree. Marge said, "This is my favorite tradition." "Go ahead Nancy, read your poems."

Nancy read for about an hour, the others listening and enjoying Nancy's words. When she finished, they all huddled together in a big family hug in front of the glowing Christmas tree. Bill and Marge went to bed and the girls sat on the floor and talked for another hour before they turned in for the night.

Sarah hummed a few Christmas songs as she prepared for bed. Within a minute of lying down I heard her calling to me, "Daniel?" "Where are you?" "Please hear me and let me hear you." I felt I could no longer remain silent and said, "I'm here, Sarah."

"Daniel, I've waited so long to hear you again." "I didn't even know if you could hear me." "Oh Daniel, I have so many questions."

"I've heard you for a very long time, Sarah." "I was unable to answer because I wasn't sure if I should." "There are many questions I might not be able to answer." "But if it is possible, I will."

"Daniel, are you an angel?"

"Well, Sarah, some people would consider me an angel." "But actually I'm just a person like you or anyone else."

"Then you aren't from heaven, Daniel?"

"In a sense, I am from heaven." "I come from a place that I consider heaven."

"I have felt your presence for a very long time." "Have you been here a long time?"

"I arrived shortly before you were born, Sarah." "I have been here ever since."

"Why did you come here, Daniel?" "Is there some special purpose for you being here?"

"I was sent to watch over you Sarah."

"Watch over me?" "Why?" "How?"

"That is something I can't tell you, Sarah." "The day will come when you will know all the answers." "All I am able to tell you is that I am here for you."

"That's fair enough, I suppose." "But how do I know

about you and it seems no one else does?" "Am I some sort of freak or something?"

"Oh, Sarah." "You're not a freak, you are special." "I don't know of anyone else that has ever had the talent you possess." "Somehow you were either born with these special abilities or have developed them over time."

"I don't feel special." "I know in the past that I would sense you and the others, but no one else seemed to be able to." "I used to think everybody could actually see you." "I thought I sensed you only because I was blind and couldn't see you like I thought everyone else could." "I finally realized no one else could see you and that only I could sense your presence." "I also sensed turmoil for you when I reacted to sensing someone." "That's when I decided to start trying to communicate this way." "This way only you and I know." "We are the only ones that know, aren't we?" "I don't want to cause trouble and I don't want you to leave me." "Does David know?"

"I think we are the only ones that know." "If David knew, I am sure I would hear about it and possibly be recalled." "I don't want to leave you either, Sarah." "I debated all of this for a very long time and decided that communicating with you this way is the best thing to do." "I can't explain why, I just feel it is what must be done."

"Can you tell me what heaven is like, Daniel?" "Can you describe it to me?"

"The only thing I can say is that it is very wonderful and beautiful, Sarah."

Soon Sarah began fading from my mind, something she

must have sensed. I heard a faint, "It seems time is up for tonight, Daniel." "I feel you slipping away." "I will try to talk to you tomorrow night." "I love you, Daniel." I said, "I love you, Sarah." not knowing if she heard me.

Each night thereafter, Sarah and I would communicate briefly. After a few months Sarah seemed to lose her ability and it would be a few nights in between communicating. She explained to me one evening that it seemed to drain her too much. We decided to communicate only once a week in order for her to avoid over extending herself. We both enjoyed the talks we had and always looked forward to the next time we could communicate.

On Sarah's 23rd birthday, she gave me quite a surprise. Her party was small and brief. She opened her gifts and shared cake with her family. She had requested a small party with only her parents and Nancy. I was to find out later why she did this. Toward sundown, she excused herself by saying, "I think I'll go for a short walk." Nancy immediately offered to walk along with her but Sarah said, "I want to think a bit." "I hope you don't mind, but I think I would just like to be alone for awhile." Sarah then left the house and slowly walked until she was at the entrance of the old storm cellar. She then turned and faced to the West.

"Please describe the sunset to me, Daniel." entered my mind. I was totally taken by surprise and said, "Sarah, I can hear you." "Are you able to communicate at any time now?" She explained to me that she had been training herself to communicate at will and used the rest she had between our weekly talks to attempt it. That is why she wanted a small party. She wanted to try and communicate with me on her birthday, a gift to me. She explained. "I was hoping I could do it and now I know I can." "But I don't know how long it will last." "So please Daniel, describe the sunset for me."

I began by describing how the clouds were layered and stretched across the horizon. They flowed together and were blended with the colors from the sun. Deep red and light orange colors mixed and swirled together in the clouds. The red of the sun mixed with the deep blue sky creating amazing purples. Sarah stood motionless, listening to me. I described how the darkness of the night was slowly creeping toward the horizon, allowing the stars to begin to shine. The sun finally sank out of sight and the night followed it across the horizon.

Sarah then approached until she was just inches away from me. "That was a wonderful description, Daniel." "I could really visualize what you were describing." "Thank you." She continued talking for awhile, reminiscing about the day Donald had stood with her at this spot. She began fading from my mind as she said, "I wish it had been you asking me to marry you that day." I barely heard her fading words, "I would have said yes to you."

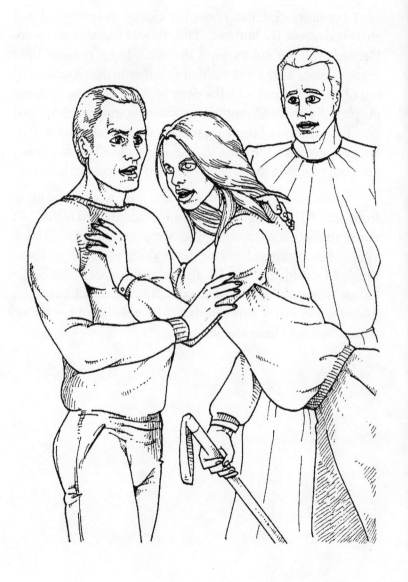

Expanded Love

It wasn't until ten days later that I once again heard from Sarah. The talk we had on her birthday had drained her completely. Over time she was able to communicate more frequently and at various times. Her ability was growing steadily stronger. By the time Summer arrived she was communicating with me briefly at least twice a day. Not only was she growing in her telepathic power, her sensing ability had focused sharply toward me. This was evident during an event that occurred at the airport.

Sarah and Nancy were going to Los Angeles to attend a scheduled speaking and book signing engagement. They arrived at the airport early, checked their luggage, and had obtained their seat assignments. Since they still had about an hour till boarding time, they decided to get something to drink at an airport restaurant. A neat, well dressed waitress directed them to an empty booth and took their drink order. A moment later I saw something that completely startled me.

The waitress was seating a man directly across from Sarah. He had a clear view of her. I could hardly contain myself because the man was ME!

Memories of that event came flooding back to my mind. I started remembering that day in my Pre-Life in great detail. I also had arrived at the airport early and had already checked in. I too had decided to spend the extra time having a drink. I was going to Washington D.C. for a job interview. It was a job that would change my direction in life. I still couldn't believe what was happening in the present.

I began to remember myself sitting in the restaurant and admiring a very beautiful girl. I now knew that girl was Sarah. I also recalled how my heart went out to her, both because of her beauty and her blindness. My Pre-Life and current feelings for Sarah merged together creating a burst of warmth within my heart and soul. I had never felt such pure love for anyone before.

Sarah attracted my attention by saying, "What is it, Daniel?" "Are you okay?" "I feel something is happening to you." "Please answer me, Daniel." What could I say to her? I couldn't tell her what was happening without revealing my Pre-Life presence sitting so close to her. I finally answered, "I'm just remembering something that happened a long time ago, Sarah." "Something very pleasant that I had completely forgotten about." She replied, "I feel a strong love coming from you." "Something here or about this place is causing your love for me to grow." "Please tell me what it is, Daniel." I tried explaining to her that I couldn't tell her what was happening without revealing things she must not yet know. She was very hard to convince.

Our conversation was interrupted when Nancy said, "We need to be heading to our gate, Sarah." I continued to try to convince Sarah that it was impossible for me to tell her what was happening to me. Finally, she gave up and told Nancy, "Okay, let's get going Nancy." As they were leaving, so was my Pre-Life self. I saw myself standing behind Sarah at the register, waiting to pay the restaurant bill. Her odor came to my memory and I felt as if I could actually smell Sarah's sweet scent. It was as if I was back in my Pre-Life, actually smelling her. Then I began to remember something else. My memory was playing through my mind at the same time events were unfolding before my eyes. I both remembered and saw Sarah turn to leave, stumbling on a frayed edge of the worn carpet. I saw and felt myself reaching out and avoiding her fall by catching her in my arms. I remembered how she felt in my arms. It was a warm and wonderful feeling flooding through me. I could feel her! In my ears and in my mind I heard the thank you from Sarah and the small talk that followed. I recalled how I watched her walk away and out of my life. I also remembered the loneliness I felt once she turned the corner and was gone from sight.

After the airplane had departed, Sarah and Nancy began talking about her near fall. Nancy commented that the man at the restaurant, the Pre-Life me, was very nice and polite. Nancy giggled and said, "I think he really liked you, Sarah." At the same moment Nancy uttered those words a look of realization came over Sarah's face. In my mind I heard her say, "Daniel, that man was YOU!" "That's what was causing the things I sensed from you." "Oh Daniel, I actually touched and talked to you in person." "I wish you had told me." "Why didn't or couldn't you tell me?"

I replied, "I couldn't tell you, Sarah." "I didn't remember the event until it happened." "It brought my complete love for you to the surface." "Our meeting was a coincidence and our life together in this world was not meant to be." "Somehow fate has brought us together in a different way." "I now know for certain that we will be together forever." "Oh Sarah, I love you and I am filled with joy and happiness."

I realized at that moment that Sarah's selection as my Chosen was pre-planned in some way. We were meant to come together in this fashion for some unknown reason. I also knew that nothing would take me away from my mission of capturing Sarah and carrying her to the New World and our future together.

Eventually, Sarah was able to communicate with me any time she wanted and anytime I spoke she could hear me. Any loneliness I had felt in the past was completely erased by Sarah. We would talk about many things and even laugh together. Sarah would always know where I was through her sensing ability. She told me she could feel my warmth and would attempt to come as close as she could without actually passing through me. She had accidentally done that once and said it felt like she had gone through a wall of warm jelly.

Time seemed to pass quickly for us and soon Sarah celebrated her 25th birthday. This was the third time we shared a sunset together. She said it was a tradition for us to walk out to the storm cellar for me to describe the sunset for her. I knew this would be the last time we would do this. In just a little over two months Sarah would be leaving this world. I think she sensed her time was nearing.

This time Sarah asked me to describe the sunset in as

much detail as I could. She told me, "Describe everything, Daniel." "Tell me how the landscape looks." "I want to envision every last detail of this sunset."

I tried as best as I could, describing the clouds, the colors and the shadows. Everything I could see I described to her. I told her about the birds soaring, silhouetted against the colors of the sunset. I described the wind moving the grass like waves on the ocean. I included how her own shadow was lengthening toward the east as the sun sank in the west. I told her about the brief flash from the sun as the top edge met the horizon. Then the shadows became one and darkness surrounded everything.

When I finished, I noticed tears running down her cheeks. She whispered, "I'm going to miss doing this." Then to my mind she said, "I'm so happy, Daniel." "Next time I will be describing the sunset for you." She slowly approached me and stopped as she barely touched me. She said to me, "I love you with all my heart and soul." "I know everything will work for us." I encircled her with my arms, barely touching her and said, "I love you and always will." "I will always be with you, Sarah."

Death and New Life

Sarah's last day was extremely busy. I hadn't heard anything from her in more than a week and knew something was wrong with her. Donald noticed it also. They both had just returned to Chicago from a tiring New York speaking engagement. Donald commented, "Sarah, you look so tired." "Are you okay?" Sarah was lying on her hotel room bed with a cold towel lying across her forehead and replied quietly, "Just a bit of a headache, Donald." "I'll be ready for the dinner tonight." "I just need to relax and sleep for a little while." Donald left as Sarah fell asleep.

I couldn't stop thinking that today was June 21, 1980 Sarah's time in this world was getting short. I tried to stay as close to her as I could. I knew something was going to happen to her very soon. I didn't know what it would be or when. The only thing I knew for certain was that Sarah would die tomorrow morning.

Sarah was to receive an award that evening from the

Chicago Children's Foundation for her selfless work with children. The dinner was scheduled to begin at 8 o'clock that evening.

It was late afternoon when Sarah awoke from her nap. She had just finished her shower when a knock came at her door. Sarah tiredly asked, "Who is it?" as she donned her robe. "It's Donald." came the muffled response through the door. Sarah seemed to stagger a bit as she walked to the door. Her hand was trembling as she found the door knob and slowly turned it. She appeared very weak. Donald saw her disorientation as soon as she opened the door. "Sarah, what's wrong?" he asked. Sarah slowly mumbled, "I don't know." "I feel so weak." She swayed as she spoke and then fainted. Donald quickly caught her and carried her to the bed. He picked up the phone and dialed for help.

Sarah was lying motionless in the hospital bed. She was very pale. Bill and Marge had driven to the hospital as soon as they received the phone call from Donald and had arrived a few hours previously. Donald Gray was sitting on the edge of the bed, holding Sarah's hand, crying. John Wilson sat in a chair in a corner of the room, holding his head in his hands, weeping. Bill and Marge sat opposite Donald, both sitting in chairs, their foreheads resting on the side of the bed. Both were crying uncontrollably. The doctor had left a moment before. He had just informed all of them of the fate of Sarah Jean Robinson.

The doctor explained that the injury Sarah suffered when she was a small girl had caused a scar inside her brain. That scar had now dissolved, rupturing a major blood vessel. The rupture and subsequent bleeding had caused extreme brain damage. He explained that there was nothing to be done. He estimated that Sarah would never regain consciousness and would be lucky to survive for a few more hours.

Nancy had remained in New York to arrange for the building of another Angel Nanna school. When she received word of Sarah's collapse, she immediately canceled all her appointments and arranged a flight to Chicago. "Please let her live." she silently said as she sat awaiting her flight.

Nancy learned of Sarah's real condition when she met John at O'Hare airport. John Wilson was waiting for her and explained what the doctor had said. Nancy began crying and John held her close. Nancy quickly regained her composure and said, "There isn't much time, let's get to the hospital before it's too late."

John and Nancy quietly entered Sarah's room and Nancy approached Sarah's bed, tears streaming down her face. She leaned over Sarah, hugging her, her head lying on Sarah's chest. Everyone was startled when Sarah said, "Don't cry Nancy." They all gathered around her bed and signaled for the nurse.

Sarah's voice was very low and weak as she said, "Don't worry, everything will be okay." "I will be leaving soon, but there is nothing to worry about." "Nanna and Daniel will take care of me." I glanced at my chronometer as the nurse entered the room. 08:33 glowed brightly, only 14 minutes left in this life for Sarah. The nurse quickly examined Sarah and left to find the doctor. Sarah continued, "Please Nancy, take care of the foundation and the children." "Mom, Dad, please take care of Nancy." "She is your only daughter now." Everyone remained silent, listening to Sarah. "Donald, help Nancy with everything." "Don't let the children down."

At 08:35, I requested the Capture Chamber. It was in my hands a minute later and I began my preparations to capture Sarah. I had just finished when Sarah called to me, "Daniel, I am nearly ready." "I know you will be successful."

A few minutes later the doctor entered and examined Sarah. He asked, "Sarah, how do you feel?" She responded, "I'm very tired, I'm leaving soon." Sarah once again told everyone not to worry and to make sure the foundation continued to help the children. By the time she finished it was 08:45, two minutes left!

Sarah's next remarks were not totally understood by the people in the room. They all just stood there, trying to comprehend. Sarah said, "Jackie, Samantha, continue to care for my parents and ease their pain." "Simone, you weren't here long but thank you for being there for me." "Nanna, I love you and will be with you soon." "William, continue to be at Nancy's side." "Give her strength and guide her." "David, you have been ever silent and watching." "I thank you for giving of yourself for my sake." Sarah then told everyone her final story:

I sat crying, feeling bad about myself. My life seemed useless and I could find no reason to go on. I had a brief thought that if I had someone who cared for me, I would be all right. It seemed I had a dark and cold life. Suddenly, warmness and light seemed to fill me, lifting my spirits. I began to feel I was truly worth something. I was filled with a feeling that I must accomplish something with my life. Life now had meaning and purpose. I no longer sat crying. Now I stood with my head held high. I felt good about myself and others. I felt a presence near me from that day forward. The presence lifted me and guided me. I finally had someone that cared for me. An Angel entered my life on that day so long ago. My Angel has been with me a very long time. My life is nearly over now and I will see My Angel soon. Thank you for your strength, warmness and your love, My Angel. I am ready to join you. Take my hand, My Angel so I may walk with you into heaven.

08:46, one minute! I hurriedly passed through Marge as I positioned myself over Sarah. She gazed up toward me and said, "Oh, Daniel, thank you the most of all." "I love you so much." "Place your hands over my heart and carry me away with you." At that, she placed her hand across her chest and said, "Here Daniel, place your hands here." I placed the Capture Chamber where Sarah's hand lay. Then she said, "Good-bye everyone, I love you all." 08:47 glowed brightly and slowly flashed. Sarah's last breath escaped as she said, "Now Daniel."

The chamber indicator glowed a bright green. I said, "Oh Sarah." "I have you Sarah." I backed off the bed, clutching the chamber tightly against my chest. I then gazed upon the empty shell that had once been Sarah. A peaceful, content look was on her face. The doctor announced, "She's gone, I'm very sorry." Marge placed her face into Bill's shoulder, crying uncontrollably. Bill held her close, soaking her cheek with his own tears. The others were holding one another, also crying in each other's arms. I stood silently, feeling their loss. I held Sarah close to me as my chronometer ticked away the final second. The room blurred before my eyes and disappeared into nothingness.

I felt as if I were being lifted. The sensation lasted momentarily and I found myself staring at Sarah's body lying in front of me. I was now in the Birth Place. I saw Nanna appear to the side of the bed where Sarah's New Life body was lying. I walked to the side opposite Nanna, placed the Capture Chamber on Sarah's chest, and pressed the release button.

Sarah gasped as she inhaled. Her eyes opened and she sat upright. She looked at me and said, "Daniel, I can see you." "I can see!" She threw her arms around me as I lifted her from the bed. She placed her feet on the shiny floor and said, "It's all so beautiful." Then she saw Nanna. She excitedly said, "Nanna!" and ran to hug her great-grandmother.

Suddenly, the room grew intensely bright. I squinted my eyes because of the brightness and immediately knew what it was. As the thought passed through my mind, Sarah said, "It's The Fathers!" They spoke as one, "Daniel, you have done well." "We know of your communication with Sarah and of her special gift." "We are pleased with both of you." "Love such as yours and hers is unique in the universe." "Be at peace and spend eternity loving one another."

The brightness faded as the words echoed in my ears. I saw my Saver and Guide, Robert, approaching. "The Searcher Counsel sent me." he said as he hugged me. He explained to me that I had been reassigned. He continued, "You are now a Caretaker, Daniel." "The Fathers are making Sarah a Caretaker also." Robert told us that we would be assigned only to children in need. Sarah and I would be working together as a team, something never done before. Even when more than one Caretaker was assigned, they were always sent separately. The Fathers made an exception for me and Sarah. We would be together on every assignment. It was a dream come true for both of us.

I fulfilled my role as Guide and Sarah learned quickly. We have been together in the New World for over 10 years and have just received our first assignment. Sarah is excited and very anxious to get started. We have our love and also a purpose. We will now spend eternity together providing strength and warmth to children in need. "Let's go help the children, Daniel." she said, holding my hand, waiting for the counter to reach zero.

ABOUT THE AUTHOR

Mr. Roberson was born in LaSalle, Illinois and spent most of his life in Central Illinois. He has an A.A.S. in Data Processing from Parkland Community College and a B.A. from Eastern Illinois University. He has three children and three grandchildren.

After graduation from LaSalle-Peru high school, Mr. Roberson joined the U.S. Air Force, where he served for nine years. He left the military in 1980 and continued working for the government as a civilian.

Soul Searchers is a concept Mr. Roberson formulated nearly seven years ago. However, it wasn't until August 1996 that he actually began writing the story.

Mr. Roberson, until recently, worked as a Computer Specialist for the Department of the Air Force. Although he did an excellent job for the government, he felt out of place. It took time, but he finally realized a higher authority was calling to him.

Mr. Roberson was compelled by this higher authority to leave his job and begin the task of getting his story completed and published. Soul Searchers, "The First Mission", is the result of his efforts and the path destiny has set for him.

Mr. Roberson is currently writing a second book dealing with Soul Searchers. He also continues to write poetry for his stories and will publish all of his poems in the near future.

Available in June 1997: Soul Searchers, "Battle of Darkness".

We know you enjoyed "The First Mission" and thank you for taking the time to read it. SO, what's next you ask? Well, the answer is "Battle of Darkness", another Soul Searcher saga involving Daniel and Sarah, other New World souls, and evil forces from the Dark Zone.

Books make excellent gifts and Soul Searchers is the type of book anyone would enjoy.

Place orders as gifts to family and friends! Just send a check or money order payable to "Destiny Publishing" along with the name and address of the person you wish to receive the book.

Cost: "The First Mission".....................................$8.99

Sales tax 4.5% (Arkansas residents only)...............$0.41

Shipping and Handling (each book ordered)...........$2.00

TOTAL Arkansas residents.................................$11.40

TOTAL Non-Arkansas residents..........................$10.99

Send to:

Destiny Publishing

P.O. Box 94436

North Little Rock, AR 72190

Please allow 4-6 weeks for delivery.